HOW TO SURVIVE IN RATION BOOK BRITAIN

I dedicate this book to my parents, Joyce and Albert 'Lofty' Botting, my grandmother, Amy Thomas, and all the other unsung heroes and heroines who kept calm and carried on throughout the war and the privations of rationing: an inspiration to us all.

HOW TO SURVIVE IN RATION BOOK BRITAIN

TONI MOUNT

First published in Great Britain in 2025 by
PEN AND SWORD HISTORY
An imprint of
Pen & Sword Books Ltd
Yorkshire – Philadelphia

ISBN 978 1 03611 762 7

A CIP catalogue record for this book is available from the British Library.

Typeset in Times New Roman 12/16 by
SJmagic DESIGN SERVICES, India.
Printed and bound in the UK by CPI Group (UK) Ltd.

The Publisher's authorised representative in the EU for product safety is
Authorised Rep Compliance Ltd., Ground Floor, 71 Lower Baggot Street,
Dublin D02 P593, Ireland.
www.arccompliance.com

For a complete list of Pen & Sword titles please contact
PEN & SWORD BOOKS LIMITED
George House, Units 12 & 13, Beevor Street, Off Pontefract Road,
Barnsley, South Yorkshire, S71 1HN, England
E-mail: enquiries@pen-and-sword.co.uk
Website: www.pen-and-sword.co.uk

or

PEN AND SWORD BOOKS
1950 Lawrence Rd, Havertown, PA 19083, USA
E-mail: uspen-and-sword@casematepublishers.com
Website: www.penandswordbooks.com

Contents

Acknowledgements		viii
Chapter 1	**Introduction**	1
	Preparing civilians for war	5
	What will I need?	7
	Funny money	8
	How will things look?	9
	Could I manage the stress?	13
Chapter 2	**Where Would I Live?**	17
	Housework	20
	Laundry	21
	Cost of living	24
	Refugees and evacuees	25
	Prefabs	31
	Utility furniture	33
Chapter 3	**What Would I Eat?**	35
	Ration books and calories	35
	Shopping	38
	Growing your own	41
	Cooking	47
	Eating away from home	53
Chapter 4	**How Can I Keep Healthy and Safe?**	56
	Getting your vitamins	56
	Free fare from the hedgerows	58
	Staying healthy	61

	Girls only	65
	Keeping safe	67
	Attack from above	68
	Air-raid shelters	73
Chapter 5	**What Jobs Could I Do?**	77
	Conscription of women	79
	Conscription of men	94
Chapter 6	**What Would I Wear?**	98
	Clothes rationing	99
	Babies' and childrenswear	100
	Fashion goes on the ration	102
	Which items are indispensable?	104
	Accessories	105
	Underwear	106
	Menswear	107
	Utility clothing	108
	Beauty is your duty	112
Chapter 7	**How Could I Keep Calm and Carry On?**	118
	Recreation	119
	Celebrations	130
	Keeping up morale	139
Chapter 8	**How Could I Do My Bit to Support the War Effort?**	140
	Recycling	140
	Warship Weeks	142
	Make Do and Mend	144
	Avoid loose talk	146
	Holidays at home	148
	The Women's Voluntary Service	150
	The Navy, Army and Air Force Institutes	151

	Other job opportunities for women	153
	The General Post Office	155
Chapter 9	**Strange But True**	158
	What about our pets?	158
	Strange ideas to cope with the blackout	163
	The strange things people do	166
	Deceiving the enemy	170
	Recycling – more strange stories	174
	Double British Summer Time	175
Chapter 10	**When Will It End?**	176
	Things can only get better	179
	Getting back to normal	184
Conclusion		186
Notes		187
Bibliography		194
Index		197

Acknowledgements

So many people were willing to share their stories of life 'on the ration' and contribute fascinating information to this book that I can only hope I have remembered to thank them all and give them the credit they deserve. Without their contributions, what a dull read this could have been. My living sources are Wendy Ahl, Christine Beech, Marion Cashman, Christine Cottrell, Kate Haines, Sue Jeeves, Richard Miller, Christine Sherman and Annie Tomkins as well as the re-enactors Jacquie Leppert and Linda Gorman at the Old Forge War Time House, Sittingbourne, Kent.

And I must mention my parents, Joyce and Albert 'Lofty' Botting, and my grandmother, Amy Thomas, who, though no longer with us, told me their marvellous tales years ago and inspired this work.

I especially have to thank my husband Glenn for all his roles as chauffeur, photographer, technical adviser, saviour from IT glitches, financial manager, general assistant and tea boy. You know I couldn't have done it without you.

Chapter 1

Introduction

This handy guide, *How to Survive in Ration Book Britain*, is intended to help those time travellers among you who wish to journey back to Britain in the mid-twentieth century, between 1939 and 1954. I should warn you that this is not an easy time. For much of the period, from 1939 to 1945, the country is involved in World War II and even after victory is achieved, Britain is cash-strapped and broke and years of austerity follow for everyone. Throughout, food, clothing, fuel, furniture and many items of everyday life we take for granted today are rationed, making it difficult to get by without scrimping, scraping and using a good deal of imagination.

During the war, people have to contend with cities, towns and even villages being bombed, lives lost and homes destroyed. Families are frequently split up as the men are called up to serve the country and children evacuated to the relative safety of the countryside. Women are expected to 'do their bit' on what is called the 'home front', maintaining the house as a place of welcome and boosting morale, stretching a few meagre food allowances to keep everyone fed and fit. This is no time for the easy life but, somehow, people manage to find lighter moments and are able to 'carry on carrying on'. You have to admire their spirit. The chances are that whatever the disaster, somebody will find a way to get a kettle boiling and make a pot of tea. The English in particular regard a 'cuppa' as the answer to just about every problem, so you'd best get a taste for it, brewed strong with sugar and milk added, if available.

After the Japanese bomb Pearl Harbor, an important United States naval base in Hawaii, in December 1941, the Americans join the war in 1942 on the side of Britain and her allies. Later that year, many

Even during the Blitz, a 'cuppa' is the answer. https://anglotopia.net/british-history/guest-long-read-voices-blitz

American troops are sent to England to help fight the war in Europe. They are known as GIs – or 'Government Issue' – which makes them sound a bit like saving stamps but these are good guys sent to a foreign country. Just how foreign Britain will seem to them is the subject of a handbook, *Instructions for American Servicemen in Britain, 1942*, published by the War Department in Washington DC. The British themselves find some parts of the booklet hilarious, as in this extract:

> Don't be misled by the British tendency to be soft-spoken and polite. If they need to be, they can be plenty tough. The English language didn't spread across the oceans

> and over the mountains and jungles and swamps of the world because these people were panty-waists.

Panty-waists? That's a new one on me. However, much of the advice given is perfect as an introduction to wartime Britain for visitors from anywhere, including you from the future. Living here can seem as different to us from the twenty-first century as it does to the Americans and the booklet puts this into context:

> Britain may look a little shop-worn and grimy to you. The British people are anxious to have you know that you are not seeing their country at its best. There's been a war on since 1939. Houses haven't been painted because factories are not making paint – they're making planes. The famous English gardens and parks are either unkept [sic] because there are no men to take care of them, or they are being used to grow needed vegetables. British taxicabs look antique because Britain makes tanks for herself and Russia and hasn't time to make new cars. British trains are cold because power is needed for industry, not for heating. There are no luxury dining cars on trains because total war effort has no place for such frills. The British people are anxious for you to know that in normal times Britain looks much prettier, cleaner, neater.

Top Tip

For GIs – Don't say 'You look like a bum'. To the British, this means you look like your own backside, not just that you're a bit scruffy. Instead of railroads, automobiles and radios, the British talk about railways, motorcars and wireless sets. If you stand in line to buy a ticket or go to the movies (cinema) you will be queuing (pro. 'cueing').

That definition of 'queuing' applies to everyone throughout this period in Britain. I'm afraid you'll have to get used to it. I suggest wearing comfortable shoes and a warm, waterproof coat for this endless outdoor activity. Take along a book to read to pass the time or chat to those either side of you in the queue. Complaints about the weather are a good, neutral topic to start with that won't get you into trouble: too hot/cold; too wet/dry; too windy/foggy, etc. 'Raining cats and dogs' means a real downpour; a 'pea-souper' is a very thick fog usually in cities with high industrial pollution.

But, in wartime, fog is often welcome as German planes can't fly to bomb their targets. However, seeing your way may be impossible. There are few, if any, streetlights because of the blackout (see below), shop signs and public buildings are unlit and vehicle headlights are reduced to faint strips of light for the same reason, so are useless in dense fog. Buses and trains have lighting reduced to a minimum, just enough to see to find a seat and, on buses, to sort out the coins to pay the conductor or, more likely, the conductress. On trains, you buy your ticket before boarding.

A pea-souper fog. BBC

From sunset until sunrise, 'blackout' is compulsory for everyone, even royalty. All windows, doorways and any other openings must be covered so that not the slightest glimmer of light can be seen from the outside. Any sign of light observed from the air may indicate buildings below to an enemy bomber pilot and thus make them a target for destruction.

Preparing civilians for war

Before war was declared on 3 September 1939, every household received Civil Defence Public Instruction Leaflet No. 2 with information on making the house light-proof, where to buy suitable cloth for blackout curtains and how to make them. The leaflet advised boarding up the windows of rooms that were rarely used and blue or black light bulbs became available to give minimal light to see by. Painting windows and skylights black was another option. Putting crosses of sticky tape of some kind on each windowpane was a precaution against flying splinters of glass, in case a bomb fell close by.

Between July and August 1939, a series of five civil defence leaflets was delivered, each dealing with a different aspect of public safety.

> Civil Defence Public Information Leaflet No. 1: Some Things You Should Know If War Should Come – Air raid warnings, gas masks, lighting restrictions, fire precautions, evacuation, food and instructions to the public in case of emergency. (6 July 1939)

> Civil Defence Public Information Leaflet No. 2: Your Gas Mask – How to store it, how to put it on and take it off. Putting your mask away. Masking Your Windows. (15 July 1939)

> Civil Defence Public Information Leaflet No. 3: Evacuation – Why and How? The Government Evacuation Scheme. What you have to do – schoolchildren, children under five, expectant mothers, the blind. Private arrangements. Work must go on. (24 July 1939)
>
> Civil Defence Public Information Leaflet No. 4: Your Food in War Time – What the government have done. How you can help. Food supplies for evacuation. National housekeeping in war time, general control, local distribution, rationing scheme. (July 1939)
>
> Civil Defence Public Information Leaflet No. 5: Fire Precautions in War Time – What might happen in war, home fire fighters, the fire bomb, how to deal with a fire, how to deal with a bomb, what you should do now. (August 1939)

As you'll realise, by that summer, war was reckoned to be inevitable.

Any blackout infringements will be met with the local ARP (Air Raid Precaution) Warden shouting 'Put that light out!' These matters are taken very seriously. Neighbours report neighbours who break the blackout rules and this isn't petty spite because everyone's life is at stake if bombs fall. Fines and even a prison term can result, if the authorities think you're flouting the law deliberately to guide enemy planes to their target. For this reason, as a new visitor, you'll need to be aware of these things.

On the whole, when in doubt, as it says in the GI's Instructions:

> The best authority on all problems is the nearest 'bobby' (policeman) in his steel helmet. British police are proud of being able to answer almost any question under the sun. They're not in a hurry and they'll take plenty of time to talk to you.

What will I need?

Before you travel back to war-torn Britain, unlike any other period previously, you will need some compulsory paperwork. An ID card is vital to prove who you are and where you live, to make certain you're not a foreign spy – blue ones for adults; brown if you're under 16 – and you'll need a ration book (see Chapter 3), otherwise you can't buy food and that includes meals or snacks from cafés, restaurants and hotels, as well as foodstuffs from shops. If you're hoping to move around the country, you must have a travel permit and if you are fortunate enough to be able to use a car, you'll require a driving licence, a driving permit and petrol is severely rationed so you have to have coupons to get it. You may even have to show a permit to enter your place of work.

The admin required for so much paperwork must be mindboggling but it seems to work well – without any computers! – just typists and filing cabinets. Even top-secret establishments rely on typists and

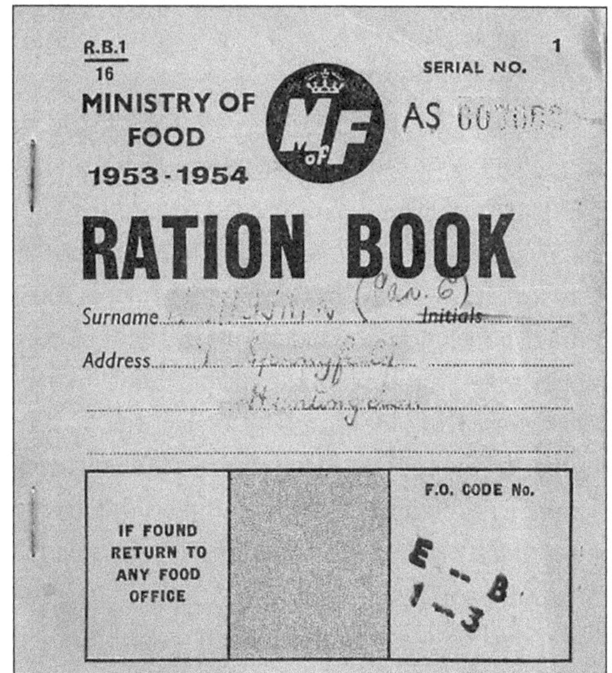

A World War II ration book. Cambridgeshire Community Archives Network

keep all their records in labelled drawers, as at Bletchley Park (see Chapter 4). Take good care of all these cards and permits because you get the first ones free but, if you lose them, replacements cost you money.

One other thing you should have with you at all times is a gas mask. At the beginning of the war, there is the fear that the enemy will drop gas grenades on the civilian population as they did on the troops in the trenches in the First World War of 1914–1918. Incidentally, this conflict is still referred to as 'The Great War' because nobody yet realises that this current war is going to be even bigger and last longer. Knowing the effects of gas can be horrific and deadly, before war is declared the government issues everyone, including tiny babies, with a gas mask and instructions on how to use it. Early on in the war, many public buildings, such as theatres, won't let you in unless you're carrying your gas mask. But as the war goes on and gas isn't used by the enemy, these rules are relaxed and eventually few bother to carry the bulky things everywhere.

Funny money

On the subject of money, Britain only began using decimal currency in February 1971, so you'll need to know all about pounds, shillings and pence. At least you've heard of pounds and pence but in the 1940s there were 240 pennies in £1, not 100. And there are some strange coins you'll need to understand. Let's start with the small copper ones. First, we have the farthing, worth ¼ of a penny. It has the head of King George VI – or George V, if it's older – and a bird, a wren, on the reverse. Then there's the halfpenny or ha'penny, worth ½ a penny which has a sailing ship on the reverse. And of course, the penny itself, which has Britannia on the reverse and twelve pennies equal one shilling.

An odd coin is the threepenny piece, known as the thrup'ny bit, which comes in two forms. One is a twelve-sided brass coin; the

> **Top Tip**
>
> Just to recap: 4 farthings or two ha'pennies equal 1d. Twelve pennies, four threepenny bits or two sixpences equal 1s. Twenty shillings equal £1. You may see prices written as 1/-, which is a shilling. Or 1/9½, which means one shilling and nine pence ha'penny. And if you should come across a large item, such as furniture or a winter coat, it may be priced in guineas. One guinea is worth £1 1s. I hope that's clear but, of course, adding up £, s, and d takes quite a bit of practice.

other is a little round silver coin. Both are worth three pennies and four equal one shilling.

My personal favourite is the silver sixpence, known as a 'tanner'. Perhaps I like it because, years after the war ended, my first pocket money was sixpence per week. It may not sound very much but, in 1960, you could buy quite a lot for 6d. Two sixpences equal a shilling. In fact, all these small denomination coins buy more than you might think, despite the local people complaining about ever-rising prices. As the old saying goes: 'Take care of the pennies and the pounds will take care of themselves.'

The silver shilling or 'bob' will buy you tea and cake with change to spare. Twenty shillings equal £1. There is also a two-shilling coin, occasionally called a 'florin', and a silver half-crown which is worth 2s 6d. There is rumoured to be a silver 'one crown' coin worth 5s but nobody has ever seen one.

Then there are the 'notes' – a ten-shilling note, a one-pound note and a five-pound note. Any higher denomination is probably a fake.

How will things look?

If you know cities like London, Liverpool and Glasgow in the twenty-first century, you will probably be shocked at what you see. Lots of people still live in Victorian buildings, some of which are now slums.

Shared outside toilets, no hot water and overcrowding contribute to dreadful housing conditions but what they lack in facilities is often overcome by incredible community spirit. Everyone knows everyone and their ability to help each other through hard times is impressive. And war makes this even more important as bombing raids reduce houses to rubble.

Before the first bomb fell, the tallest building in London was St Paul's Cathedral and, remarkably, it remains so throughout the period. The capital has no skyscrapers but some very grand buildings, many built by Victorian entrepreneurs. Some of these suffer in the Blitz. Beautiful parks and gardens are dug up to become allotments. Allotments are green areas 'allotted' to local people by the authorities to grow vegetables and fruit or even as space to keep chickens or a pig to provide extra food for all. For those without a garden of a good size, an allotment can be a lifesaver, putting food on the table.

In the countryside, the landscape is recognisable but farms tend to be smaller than in the twenty-first century and labour is more intensive and hands-on. You may see horses ploughing, pulling carts and doing other farm work. In some places, the horses have always done this but, with fuel in such short supply, horse-power sees a revival, replacing diesel-guzzling tractors for the duration of the war. Much of the farm workforce is provided by women, known as 'land girls', replacing men called up for the services.

Despite the horrors of war, the countryside is still beautiful but there are differences. Road signs which point the way to this village or that are removed. The worry is that, if the enemy actually invade, they'll be able to find their way around easily by following these signs. Railway station names have gone for the same reason, making it tricky for travellers to know when and where to get off the train.

Overhead, especially in the lovely blue skies of South East England in the summer of 1940, the Battle of Britain is being waged. Spitfires and Hurricanes have aerial 'dog fights' with enemy planes, eagerly watched and cheered on by young boys who can identify every type of aircraft as well as any RAF 'spotter'. Pieces of shrapnel – sometimes still hot from the fight – are collected as mementoes to be treasured. But, to us, this is a dire business as lives are lost in full view of those on the ground.

Constance Miles, known as Connie, keeps her journals from 24 August 1939 to 15 April 1943. She lives in the village of Shere in Surrey, close to local RAF Stations at Croydon and Biggin Hill which are heavily involved in the Battle of Britain. On Friday, 28 March

Lads collect up Battle of Britain shrapnel. Geoff Charles, National Library of Wales

1941, she notes that sometimes it is difficult to hate the enemy. This is a story she heard from a friend:

> A woman living in Sussex was suddenly told that a German aeroplane had been shot down in one of her fields. Would she come out with some brandy and rugs: a German was dying. 'No,' she said, 'I can't. I simply can't. Let him get on with his dying, the brute.' They returned. 'Do come. He is suffering so much.' 'Oh well, I suppose I must,' she said and she went to the field. All her resentment and hatred vanished at the sight of the suffering youth with his face of utter anguish. He died in her arms and his last words were 'Heil Hitler!' The young English aviator who shot him down stood nearby and was terribly affected, saying, 'I didn't think it could be half as bad as this!'[1]

The people you meet will probably be wearing out-of-style clothes that maybe patched. With clothing rationed, it's not a good 'look' to wear new items. Neatly patched, carefully darned and revamped clothes earn you more respect, showing that you're 'doing your bit' for the war effort. Recycling is the fashion statement of the time.

An interesting detail about behaviour and respect is noted in the GI's Instructions:

> Do not be offended if Britishers do not pay as full respects to national or regimental colors as Americans do. The British do not treat the flag as such an important symbol as we do.

During the war, my dad was in the Royal Navy, stationed in Iceland along with some American sailors. On one occasion, he was wiping the windows of their hut to remove the ice and the Americans were aghast when they saw the cloth he was using was an old Union Jack! The Instructions continue:

> But the British pay more frequent respect to their National Anthem. In peace or war 'God Save the King' is played at the conclusion of all public gatherings such as theater performances. The British consider it bad form not to stand at attention, even if it means missing the last bus. If you are in a hurry, leave before the National Anthem is played. That's considered alright.

Could I manage the stress?

This question is impossible to answer but, as the GI's Instructions remind the US Servicemen in 1942:

> Sixty thousand British civilians – men, women and children – have died under bombs, and yet the morale of the British is unbreakable and high. A nation doesn't come through that, if it doesn't have plain, common guts. The British are tough, strong people, and good allies.

Can you match that? Air raids mean sleepless nights, often spent in cold, cramped, uncomfortable shelters of some sort. Public shelters are *very* public; toilet facilities may be a bucket behind a screen and your fellows noisy but everyone has to rub along together and make the best of it. But it's not entirely bad news because the sense of camaraderie is strong since you are all in the same dangerous situation.

There may also be raids during the day which require you to stop whatever you're doing and rush to the nearest shelter. Despite a lack of sleep and interruptions, women in particular are persuaded to look their best, wearing make-up and keeping their hair gorgeous, to boost morale. According to the government's ideas on psychology, nothing lowers the spirits worse than a dowdy-looking female. It's very sexist, I know, but that's the way it is in the 1940s and for decades to

A London County Council Ambulance Driver 'puts on a brave face'. Imperial War Museum

come. And, at the time, women go along with this as part of their war effort. I've read that after every terrible Blitz bombing, women wear the most vivid scarlet lipstick possible because they wish to be seen to defy Hitler, who is said to severely disapprove of females with bright red lips.

Perhaps you can help boost morale by taking some bright, Hitler-defying lipsticks with you when you travel back in time because make-up, although never rationed, can be in short supply. Any female friends you make there will be delighted with such gifts.

But the GI's Instructions remind visitors that women deserve respect:

> A British woman officer can and often does give orders to a man private. The men obey smartly and know it is no shame for British women have proven themselves in this war. They have stuck to their posts near burning ammunition dumps, delivered messages afoot after their

> motorcycles have been blasted from under them. They have pulled aviators from burning planes. They have died at the gun posts and as they fell another girl has stepped directly into the position and 'carried on.' There is not a single record in this war of any British woman in uniformed service quitting her post or failing in her duty under fire. Now you understand why the British respect the women in uniform. They have won the right to the utmost respect. When you see a girl in khaki or air-force [or navy] blue with a bit of ribbon on her tunic, remember she didn't get it for knitting more socks than anyone else in Ipswich.

If you enjoy shopping in the twenty-first century, you'll find things quite different in wartime Britain. I've already mentioned queuing and money, but the odd opening hours of most shops is something you need to understand. In general, shops, cafés and restaurants are closed on Sundays and most towns and villages have an 'early closing' day, usually Wednesday or Thursday, but each place has its own tradition. Whatever the local custom, shops will close at lunchtime or, maybe, not open at all that day. With wartime shortages, not only of wares and merchandise for sale but of staff being called to do war work, shops may reduce their opening hours even further, or close if they run out of items to sell. So if you want to buy something, go early but don't be too disappointed if the shop isn't open for business, whatever day of the week it happens to be. As you'll realise, in these times, shopping isn't an enjoyable pastime but a tedious chore and usually involves waiting in queues.

Connie Miles made a list of changes she saw in her village life caused by the war on Tuesday, 13 October 1942:

> I see many army lorries packed with soldiers. Many army waggons. Often a tank and many motorcycles.
>
> I am pleased when I see a pile of scones in the teashops (they both tend to close constantly).

> I receive a tiny bit of bacon for boiling with enthusiasm at the grocer's. it is a battle to get it and one takes what is given.
>
> Many more ladies with shopping baskets.
>
> Dull, dismal blackout curtains at every window and no new paint – every house almost shabby.
>
> In the greengrocer's there are cauliflowers ten pence each, pears 1/- a pound and tomatoes 1/- a pound.[2]

But there are a few bonuses to visiting Britain at this time. As the GI's Instructions note:

> The Briton is the most law-abiding citizen in the world because the British system of justice is about the best there is. There are fewer murders, robberies and burglaries in the whole of Great Britain in a year than in a single large American city.

So that's reassuring, isn't it? But there are new dangers, of course, as the GIs are reminded:

> There are housewives in aprons and youngsters in knee-pants in Britain who have lived through more high explosives in air raids than many soldiers saw in the last war.

As you'll realise, a visit to the past at this time is going to take courage. Are you ready for it?

Chapter 2

Where Would I Live?

What sort of house you might live in depends on your income and the area of the country you choose. As I mentioned above, some cities still have slum housing which dates back to Victorian times with little, if anything, by way of amenities, sanitation or privacy. However, since the Great War, life in the suburbs has expanded.

In the Victorian and Edwardian eras, the house was the family's base. Men went out on business, women entertained visitors in the morning room or, later in the day, in the drawing room. Children were overseen by their nurse in the nursery and servants got on with their jobs. But after the First World War, society changed, domestic staff were harder to recruit and houses became smaller. A quiet revolution led to the building of suburban semi-detached houses (constructed in pairs) with the living room as the family focus. This comfortable space now serves as the hub for conversation, relaxation, reading, listening to the wireless and informal entertaining.

'For the average British man and woman, each day begins and ends in the family centre. The influence of a happy, harmonious home is therefore a national asset.' But this contemporary 1930s description of a 'national asset' is about to be disrupted by war.

Meanwhile, to you, electrical appliances are everyday items taken for granted. Flick a switch and you have light, heat, hot water and entertainment, food is mixed, blended and cooked. But in Britain in the 1930s, for some people these were new marvels. Let's talk to Mr Johnson, the sales assistant at the Electrical Showroom – yes, there is such a thing – and ask him about the latest electrical gadgets. Note how polite both customer and sales assistant should be and the

Above and below: A pair of 1930s suburban semi-detached houses, many still standing in 2024. Geograph

formal tones of address. Wives refer to their husbands as 'Mr Smith', or whatever. Courtesy like this is expected:

> 'Good morning, Mr Johnson.'
>
> 'Good morning, madam. How may I help you?'
>
> 'I saw the advertisement for "Electric Hot Water" in the newspaper and I'm interested to learn more.'
>
> 'Yes, indeed, madam. You hear more women singing over the washing up these days and they're happy because they have constant hot water in their kitchens. Away goes the grease in a cloud of steam and because they have constant hot water, they wash up as they go so the pots and plates don't accumulate. No wonder they sing: electric hot water has broken the back of the job. Wouldn't it be nice to have an electric water heater yourself?'
>
> 'Well, yes, I suppose…'
>
> 'And it's so easy and inexpensive to install and saves money all the time because it cuts off the current the instant it's not required.'
>
> 'I'll give it some thought…'
>
> 'But what about your electric lighting, madam? Has anyone in your house tripped and fallen or bumped into something, causing breakages?'
>
> 'Well, Mr Smith tripped and broke the hall lamp but that was due to seven G&Ts at the party.'
>
> 'More and better electric lights will not only make your home as accident free as possible but add enormously to your comfort and preserve your eyesight. Our new 100-watt electric lamps are so cheap and safety demands more light on stairs and landings – your eyes beg for it, madam.'
>
> 'Mm, I do read a great deal… Thank you, Mr Johnson. I'll let you know what I decide. Good morning.'
>
> 'And good morning to you, madam, and thank you. If you come back later this week, I can maybe give you a special discount on light bulbs…'[1]

Salespersons may be more polite but selling the merchandise and making money is always the point of the exercise. Even in the war years, when electric labour-saving devices aren't for sale, adverts promoting them still appear, jolting customers' memories and making it clear they will be back in stock when the war ends. In 1944, a well-known vacuum cleaner manufacturer 'salutes' the housewife who works as a bus conductress, collecting fares and advising passengers where to alight since road signs are few. But after a long day on her feet, she still has 'the hundred and one jobs a housewife can't neglect' to do when she goes home. At least, when it's down to the cleaning, 'her pre-war Hoover comes in useful and there are millions like her doing a "double job" in this war'. So let's look at some of the tasks you may need to know about, whatever sort of house you live in.

Housework

Definitely not my 'thing' but housewives of the 1940s and 1950s take this very seriously. Begin with the entrance to your home where you want to make a good first impression on visitors or even passers-by, sweeping and washing down the front path and maybe the pavement beyond if it's muddy or has been fouled by a dog. In this latter case, it prevents visitors bringing any muck on their shoes into your clean house. The porch, front door and steps need sweeping and dusting down. Brass knockers, letterboxes and step-edges should be polished daily until they gleam. Now you are ready for visitors to enter.

 **Top Tip**

When washing dirty dusters in soapy water, don't rinse out the soap before letting them dry. They'll be slightly sticky and pick up dust more efficiently. *Home Companion Magazine*, July 1943.

They're already dazzled by the entrance and, once inside, should be greeted by the scent of beeswax and furniture polish.

Shiny floors, whether wood or linoleum, should be well polished – appearance is more important than health and safety, so it seems, and using a wet rag to apply the floor polish makes it go further. Wartime magazines and helpful leaflets are full of hints like this. Adding paraffin to any polish has the same effect and, apparently, keeps flies away. But paraffin, being a fuel, may be in short supply, like the polish, and the smell is as unpleasant to humans as to flies, so I'm not sure about this idea.

Another excellent cleaning agent is cold tea. Tea comes as loose-leaf – no teabags – and the used leaves can be collected in a bucket for a week, then boiling water is added and, after an hour, strained off and bottled. This 'tea-water' is good for washing dirty hands, thus saving rationed soap, shining up mirrors, windows and glassware and, like paraffin, deters flies while smelling more pleasant. Finger-marks on wooden furniture are a problem, so says an advert for Stephenson's Superior Furniture Cream, especially for those who have evacuees staying in their homes (see below).

Laundry

With the house vacuumed, dusted and polished, what about the laundry? Monday is the traditional day for washing clothes, linens, sheets, towels, etc. This custom goes way back because the back-breaking job of doing the washing, getting it dried, aired, ironed and ready to wear, clean, to church on Sunday, can take all week, especially if the weather is bad and you can't dry it outside in this era before tumble dryers. In a 'Plan of Work for a Small Servantless House', a housewife's duties for Monday dictate:

> Brush all clothes used over the week-end and put away. Collect large articles and send to laundry or do laundry-work

> at home. If all family laundry is done at home, help may be necessary. Wash silk and woollens first, followed by white things. These can be done on alternate weeks if preferred.

'Help' might be 'necessary' but it isn't always available. I remember Mum doing all the washing for our family of four in our little terraced house. Sheets, pillow slips and towels were boiled up in the 'copper'. The copper was a boiling cylinder, filled with water from the tap by the bucketful and a gas-ring lit underneath it first thing Monday morning. The kitchen would be filling with soapy-smelling steam by breakfast time. Woollens and smaller items were washed in the deep white sink while the linens and cottons 'simmered' in the copper.

Once the small things were washed, rinsed, put through the mangle to squeeze out the water and hung on the line in the garden to dry, then came the hardest task: manhandling the sheets and towels, steaming hot, out of the top of the copper, using large wooden tongs. This was made more difficult as the copper was mounted above the bath because, on Friday nights, it was used to heat the water for everyone's weekly bath. Yes, we bathed in the kitchen, all using the same water but topping it up with hot from the copper!

The steaming sheets would go through the mangle – and if you want to build up your biceps, this job will do it – catching the hot, soapy water in a bucket as it's squeezed out and returning it to the copper for reuse, boiling soiled items like babies' nappies (when my little sister came along).

The sheets were then rinsed by hand in the sink, mangled again and pegged out to dry, weather permitting. I've known sheets to freeze stiff as cardboard on the line on a frosty morning. When just

 **Top Tip**

A wartime tip Mum still used was a cotton bag full of crushed eggshells which acted as a good bleaching agents for whites if put in the copper.

> **Top Tip**
>
> There are alternatives. Rice is a grain full of starch and you can starch washed clothes by soaking them in water in which rice has been cooked before ironing them dry. *Home Companion*, June 1943.

about dry, things would be brought indoors for ironing. It's easier to get the creases out, if they're still a bit damp and then hung on a clothes horse to finish drying in front of the fire – the only heating in the house in the living room.

Some housewives like to starch cotton and linen items like shirts, blouses and aprons. It makes them crisp, gives them a sheen and helps repel dirt. But starch is made from grain, just like flour and bread so, during the war, it's regarded as a waste of a basic food crop and is no longer produced.

All types of soap go on the ration on 9 February 1942. This is because it's manufactured using fats and oils and, like starch, these products are needed as food. But the government are sneaky about rationing soap, fearing people will stockpile supplies beforehand, leaving others without any. So the paperwork required doesn't mention 'soap' but refers to 'nutmegs'. As Lord Woolton recalled:

> Nobody was particularly interested or curious about nutmegs and there was no sign of any leakage of information on this subject until the Saturday afternoon before I was going to make the announcement [about soap rationing] on the Sunday. Then … the story leaked that nutmegs were to be rationed; reports came in … that there had been a sudden rush in the shops on nutmegs. I wonder what happened to all the nutmegs … purchased on that Saturday afternoon.

Lord Woolton is the man in charge of the Ministry of Food and we'll be meeting him again in Chapter 3.

Cost of living

Rises in the cost of living are familiar to us in the twenty-first century and you probably won't be surprised that, during the war, there is the same problem – everything is increasing in price with an average of 26 per cent in the cost of living in the fifteen months from September 1939 to January 1941. By this time, coal is 41 per cent more expensive. Saving fuel becomes a way of life, many suggestions being reinstated in the twenty-first century – lag pipes, insulate hot water tanks, turn down the heating and trying to use less electricity at peak times (this is between 8.00 am and 1.00 pm which, according to the Ministry of Fuel and Power, is the period of peak production in factories with a lesser peak between 3.00 pm and 5.00 pm).

Paper and matches for fire-lighting are in short supply – both paper and the chemicals in match-heads are used in munitions manufacture – but there are alternatives. Dried potato peelings make good kindling and strips torn from bread wrappers – in those days made from waxed paper, not plastic, to keep the bread moist – can be used as spills instead of matches 'for lighting your pipe', as one source suggests.

One huge difference you will need to get your head around is a very different scale of income. For example, in December 1944, with no sign of the war ending any time soon, *Good Housekeeping* magazine ran an article about how a newlywed housewife should budget the running of her home. The advice works out costs assuming an income

Did You Know?

One thing you are probably not familiar with as a fuel economy is the use of fire-bricks on open fires. These can be blocks of chalk, pumice stone or clay and you put them on a coal fire when it's burning well. The bricks don't burn but soak up heat and radiate it out into the room again long after the fire has gone out.

of £500 a year as an example with rent estimated as £125. This may be a reasonable guess for that of the magazine's middle-class readers but is nowhere near the lowest wage on which some have to survive.

One possible means of saving suggests cutting 'your domestic help to a minimum', but what of the wages of the domestic help? For my grandmother, Amy Thomas, a widow in her fifties, her income came from a widow's pension of a shilling a week and the money she earned cleaning the houses of 'posh' people every morning and waiting tables at a hotel in the evenings with 'tips'. For her, life was measured in shillings rather than pounds.

For you, if you're middle class, the article says that 15s a week should cover your food bill but, it warns: 'Even today it is still possible to over-spend on canned and prepared foods, biscuits, etc.'

Refugees and evacuees

Before war is declared in September 1939, trouble is already brewing across Europe. Refugees, escaping the conflict in fear of their lives, come to Britain. Homes have to be found for them, food and clothing provided and, for many, they need to learn English in order to get jobs, shop or go to school.

A young Jewish boy named Manfred Seelig escaped the Holocaust in which the rest of his family perished. He came to Britain via the Kindertransport. When he was old enough, he worked as a translator for the British Army, changing his name to Martin Fredrick Sherman. He later married a Jewish girl who had also escaped Germany on the Kindertransport.[2]

Linda Gorman, née Guess, was evacuated as a baby with her mum and 7-year-old sister from The Bull Pub at Hunton, near Maidstone in Kent, to Devon. They were taken in by a woman who, despite the three extra ration books and a weekly cash allowance for evacuees of 10/6 for the first child, 8/6 for the second, plus the same for their mother, gave them so little food, their mum became ill. She phoned her husband back in Kent – the pub had the only phone in village – and he told them to catch the train and come home and he would meet them at the station in Maidstone. They took the train from Devon to Paddington, in London, then on the Underground across London and another train back to Maidstone. But there was no one to meet them. Dad had been called to duty as a Local Defence Volunteer which took priority over family matters. So Linda's mum, though sick from lack of food, walked seven miles to Hunton village, carrying the baby and with the tired 7-year-old in tow.

Not long after, a doodlebug, a German V1 flying bomb, hit Hunton. Dad was blown across the bar of the pub while the 7-year-old sister hid under a bench. Part of the roof collapsed in the upstairs bedroom where baby Linda was sleeping. They found her covered in dust but a chunk of ceiling had come to rest, supported by the sides of the cot, and Linda was safe underneath. Mum felt guilty at bringing her daughters home and into such danger. But at least they were being properly fed.[3]

Many refugees and evacuees have tales like these, some stories of kindness, others not. Life is difficult for those who have to leave their homes but those who take them in also have to adjust to having strangers in the house and all the extra work that involves. In the early months of the war, with the expectation that London will be the prime target for enemy bombers, more than one-and-a-half million school children from the capital and surrounding areas are evacuated to the countryside in 1939 as part of Operation Pied Piper.[4]

The 'Phoney War' – when the expected enemy bombers don't come – sees London remaining free of attack until May 1940 and, during that period, many parents bring their children home again. It must be traumatic for the youngsters, most of whom have never been away from home before. Imagine being confronted by a herd of cows if you're only familiar with cats and dogs. You stay with strangers – unless you are taken in by relatives – maybe along with other evacuees you don't know and whether you are chosen by kind people or mean ones is all a matter of luck, depending on who chooses

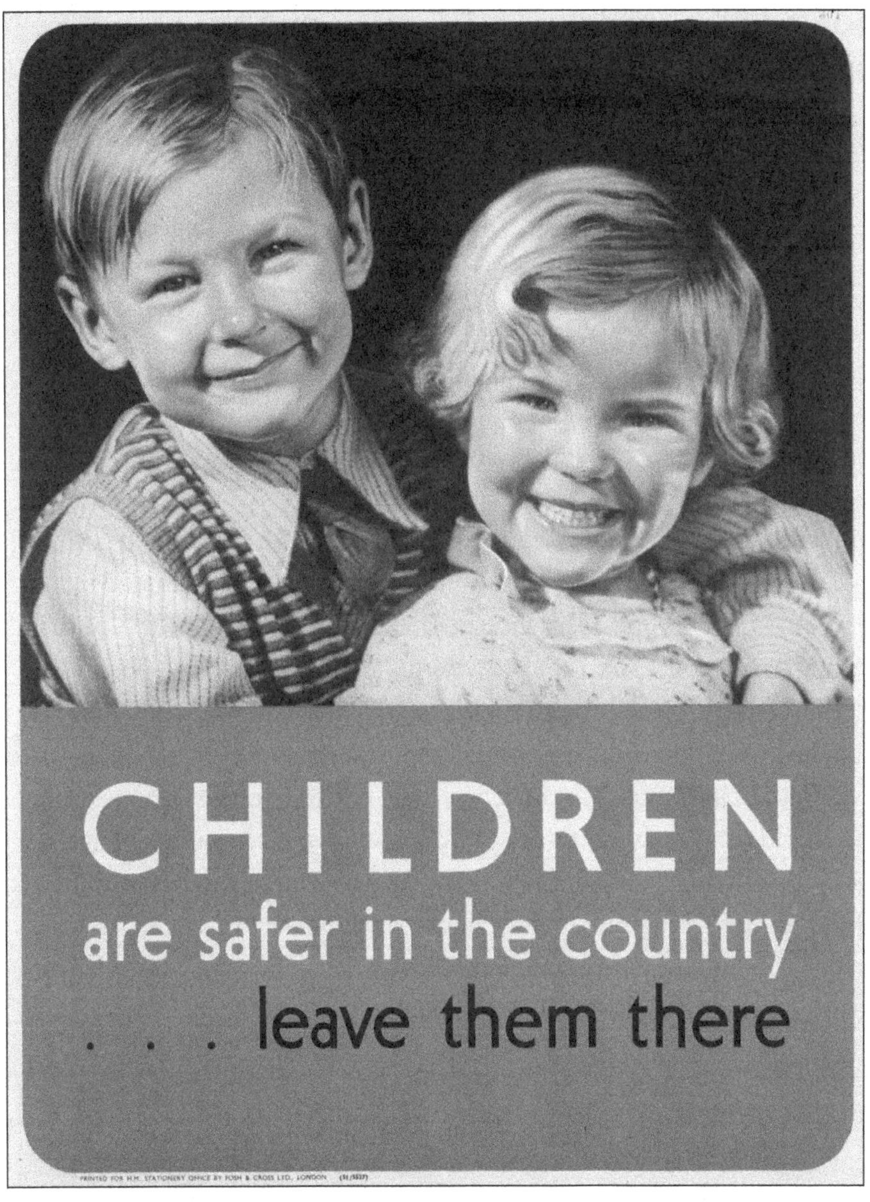

Evacuees. The National Archives & Wikicommons

you! Yes, if you are good-looking, seem healthy but not likely to eat too much, you might be chosen first. Some country folk want strong lads to help with farm chores; elderly folk might want a girl to do housework. Others want quiet, well-behaved children who won't be too much bother so they can ignore them. You may be welcomed with delight or treated as an unwanted nuisance.

On Wednesday, 8 January 1941, Connie Miles noted in her diary that:

> Mrs R is entertaining two boy evacuees from the East End [of London]. They arrived with only one of every garment. They had never used a toothbrush. Their mother, being requested to do something about it, posted one to use between them.[5]

The evacuations are done school by school in the hope that children will at least be with friends and classmates and know the teachers who are in charge of them during the long journey. They are instructed to take their gas mask, a change of underwear, night clothes, indoor shoes or plimsolls (school gym shoes), socks or stockings, a toothbrush, comb, face cloth, soap and towel, handkerchief and, if possible, a warm coat or mackintosh (a waterproof coat), along with food for the day. One small toy is allowed and it all has to fit in a bag or case which the child must carry themselves. For the poorest, the bag may be an old pillow cover. Every child must have their name and school number written on a stout label which is pinned to their coat, in case they get split up from their school party. Most evacuees are taken out of the cities by train, some by buses and a few by boat, pleasure steamers making it seem like a holiday.

Did You Know?

In the *Weekly Dispatch,* on 9 March 1941, was this snippet:

'Please teacher,' a boy asked, 'Did God make Hitler?'

'Oh yes,' the teacher assured him, 'God made Hitler.'

'Well I never did!' exclaimed the little lad and his face fell as he spoke.

From *Mrs Miles's Diary*, p. 217

From Friday, 1 September 1939, children are lined up in the school playground to walk in crocodiles to the appointed railway or Underground station or ready to board buses. Tearful mothers often escort them and some cannot bear to see their children go, pulling them aside. In fact, because it's voluntary, only one-third of eligible evacuees in London actually leave. It's the same in other cities but 40,000 children depart from Leeds in Yorkshire, an industrial, manufacturing centre in northern England, 36,000 from Liverpool and 37,000 from the Naval Dockyard area of Chatham in North Kent.[6]

Even with fewer children than expected, the logistics are incredible: every school knows which train at which station is allotted to them with groups' arrivals timed at less than fifteen-minute intervals. In London, trains depart every nine minutes between 8.30 and 5.30! But, of course, things don't always go as planned: groups arrive early or late and are simply put on the next train leaving, meaning that children who are expected in South Wales may end up in Norfolk.

On a trip through Kent, at Petts Wood, a field is dug over to make latrine pits, such as the army use. Trains stop here and the evacuees are herded out into the field for a compulsory comfort break, as one youngster recalled. Whether this 'facility' was provided elsewhere, I don't know.

Children arrive at their destination tired, hungry and dishevelled, not at their best, yet now they have their first meeting with their new guardians. The newly formed Women's Voluntary Service (the WVS, later the Women's Royal Voluntary Service) helps out at reception

Top Tip

Long journeys with youngsters are always problematic. Out-of-date railway carriages without toilets have to be used for this mass transportation and one lad recalls that the boys would pee out the window. He doesn't say how the girls managed so maybe it would be a good idea to take along an old bucket for emergencies!

points, offering food and drink. Girl Guides do their share, looking after the little ones, while Boy Scouts carry the belongings of exhausted children.

Evacuation is the parents' choice, whether to send the children away to a safer place, to live with strangers, or risk keeping them at home. However, at the other end of the chain, taking in evacuees isn't a choice. If your house has space, you are allotted a child, or maybe two or three, to house and care for as their 'billeter'.

The local schools are responsible for educating all these extra children, giving them a hot meal at midday and keeping them amused and busy. To avoid overcrowded classrooms, some schools teach their local pupils in the morning and the newcomers and their teachers use the space in the afternoon. Academic standards may fall but the evacuees have a whole new world to learn about and understand. Some are stunned to discover that milk comes from cows and doesn't originate in glass bottles; others find the lack of noise at night disturbing while star-lit skies, away from air pollution, are a revelation. Caring for livestock, learning how to plant and harvest vegetables and getting used to a whole new way of life is marvellous for some, terrifying for others. As the 'Phoney War' continues into 1940, many go home to the cities but after the Blitz begins in earnest, many return along with some who never evacuated previously.

From *Mrs Miles's Diary*, Wednesday, 1 June 1942, written about the local children and some evacuees in her village of Shere in Surrey:

> The papers say that children are to be kept at school all holidays so that the mothers may go on with their war work. This great edict must be the work of a male mind. Village children only go to school for so many hours a day and their mothers are at home, keeping house, unless there is an aunt or grannie to supervise. Very bad too for the tired teachers. The youngster[s] are conscious that something unusual is on and take advantage of it.

> They are as wild and naughty as they can be, eating together at the school kitchen in the village hall, instead of sitting quietly having lunch in their cottages. I imagine the teachers would refuse.

Prefabs

As it says in the GI's Handbook:

> The British have been bombed, night after night and month after month. Thousands of them have lost their houses, their possessions, their families. So where are those made homeless going to live?

Over 200,000 houses are destroyed by bombing during the war. If you're in this predicament, you may be re-housed in a 'prefab'. The idea becomes law in the Housing (Temporary Accommodation) Act 1944 which planned to build 300,000 prefab(ricated) houses in Britain over the next four years. In fact, just over 150,000 are built. All prefab units approved by the Ministry of Works must have a minimum floor space of 635 square feet (59.0 m^2), and be a maximum of 7.5 feet (2.3 m) wide so they can be transported by road.

After the war, the government has aircraft factories turn to manufacturing prefabricated, single-storey homes using recycled aluminium airframes from crashed planes. Other styles use a timber frame with asbestos cement infill and cladding.[7] Made in sections, these are assembled on site – sometimes a previous bomb site where houses were destroyed – in just three days, the work often being done by prisoners-of-war. These little houses are meant to be temporary accommodation, designed to last a decade while proper brick houses are constructed.

Prefabs also have indoor plumbing, bathrooms and modern kitchens, which the bombed-out houses they replace often did not.

The best innovation by the Ministry of Works is what is termed the 'service unit', something all designs should include. A service unit is a combined prefabricated kitchen that backs onto a bathroom, pre-built in a factory to an agreed size. It means that the unsightly water pipes, waste pipes and electrical cables are all in the same place and quick and easy to install.

Prefabs have coal fires but another brilliant innovation is the 'back-boiler' installed behind the fire to make constant hot water for the kitchen, bathroom and central heating – this last known to very few ordinary people previously, except for the well-off. Gone is the outside, possibly shared, lavatory and the tin bath because the bathroom includes a flushing toilet and a fitted, full-sized bath with hot running water. The kitchen has such modern luxuries as a built-in oven, refrigerator and an electric water heater, which only later become common in most homes.

And you don't have to decorate because all prefabs under the housing act come pre-decorated with magnolia walls and gloss-painted

A prefab with a garden where you can dry the washing. Flashbak.com

green woodwork, including door surrounds and skirting boards, so I hope you like the colour scheme. Each one has its own little garden plot, to be cultivated as you wish or simply as a place to dry the washing. Many inner-city houses don't have this luxury.

No wonder prefabs, so far ahead of their time, become the inhabitants' pride and joy and where many are put up together, they create new, close-knit communities. Despite only being considered 'temporary', they're so well made, many are still standing proudly, lived in and loved by their occupants into the twenty-first century in parts of the country. Some are even 'listed' as Grade II Historic Buildings to be preserved for posterity.

Utility furniture

Now many of those unfortunate enough to be 'bombed out' have a house to live in but a house needs furniture to make it a home. But you may have lost everything when the bombs dropped and now, like so much else, new furniture is hard to come by. The government's answer is 'Utility furniture'.

Timber suitable for furniture-making is scarce and factory production lines have been given over to the war effort so, by 1941, there is a shortage of new furniture. The Utility Furniture Advisory Committee is set up in 1942 to make sure that what little there is available is shared efficiently. You won't be surprised to hear that new furniture is rationed and restricted to newlyweds and those who have been bombed under the Domestic Furniture (Control of Manufacture and Supply) (No. 2) Order 1942 which comes into force on 1 November 1942.

The committee's approved designs are illustrated in the *Utility Furniture Catalogue* of 1943. Furniture is to be strong, made to last, simple in design using timber most efficiently. In the twenty-first century, these ideas are very 'on trend' but pre-war designs had been ornate and the simple, basic lines of Utility items aren't popular at

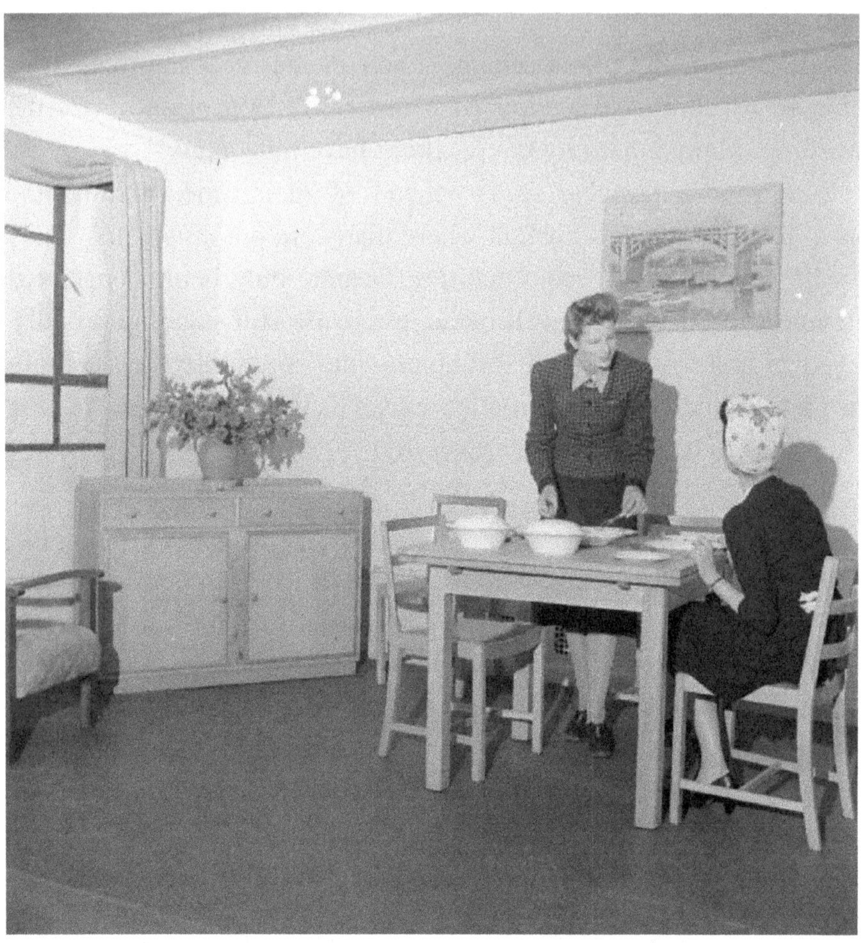

My parents, as newlyweds in 1943, had a Utility Furniture draw-leaf table, chairs and sideboard just like these which were still in daily use in the 1970s. www.furniturerentalonline.co.uk/blog/wwii-utility-furniture-and-rationing-blog

the time. They aren't appreciated any better after the war either and when furniture rationing ends in 1952, the committee is disbanded as people return to preferred, more decorative styles.

So now you have somewhere to live, furnished and decorated. You know how to keep it cosy as efficiently as possible. In the next chapter, we will look at what there is available to eat, how food rationing works and the best and most economical ways to cook in these austere times.

Chapter 3

What Would I Eat?

Ration books and calories

As you'll realise by now, in order to buy food you must have a ration book. At the beginning of the war, in January 1940, everyone is issued with their first ration book and you need a new one each year. As a visitor, until you find a permanent residence, you'll require temporary, emergency coupons to allow you to buy rationed food wherever you are. These are available from the local Food Office, which is where you get your ration book, any coupons and also your ID card. Once you know where you're living, you have to register with the local butcher and grocer and always buy your food from the same shop. And don't worry: you won't be missing out on bargains elsewhere because prices are fixed by the Ministry of Food, set up in 1940, so they're the same everywhere.

The government has been preparing for the possibility of war, having organised the Food (Defence Plans) Department back in November 1936 and ration books were printed in 1938. Lessons had been learned about food shortages during the Great War of 1914–1918 when the rich could buy as much as they wished of the best of everything while poorer people queued for hours for supplies that quickly ran out and often went hungry. This was no way to keep the general population fighting fit so rationing was designed to solve this problem of inequality.

It isn't meant to deny anybody the food they need but to share out the supplies more fairly. The overall result, surprisingly, is that those on low incomes actually eat a more nutritious diet than they did before the war. A quarter of pre-war Britons were undernourished, infant mortality was high and 80 per cent of children under 5, particularly in polluted cities, had some bone abnormality such as rickets, caused by a lack of vitamin D and sunshine. But by 1943, under the National Milk Scheme, these children are drinking three times as much milk as before the war. The Vitamin Welfare Scheme provides them with cod liver oil, full of vitamins A and D, and when supplies allow, orange juice for vitamin C. These items, as well as dried milk powder for babies, are all available at the Food Office.

Most adults receive a beige-coloured ration book but 'priority' cases – pregnant women, nursing mothers, babies and children under 5 – get green books, allowing them the first choice of any available fruit and extra orange juice, an extra pint of milk a day and twice as many eggs as the standard adult ration. Children aged between 5 and 16 have a blue book which permits fruit, a full meat ration and an extra half-pint of milk a day. The idea is that strong, fit women produce healthy children who grow into strong, fit adults for any future war effort.

In January 1940, as soon as the books are issued, bacon, butter and sugar go 'on the ration', followed by meat in March and, in May, a 'Limitation of Supply Order' restricts the production of non-essential consumer goods as factories are given over to the war effort. This leads to a shortage of soap, cosmetics and similar items. In April 1940, Lord Woolton becomes Minister of Food and under his direction rationing works efficiently. He launches a campaign against food waste with this message:

> Here is your part in the fight for Victory. When a particular food is not available, cheerfully accept something else – home produced if possible. Keep

Top Tip

One suggestion is not to throw away the water in which vegetables have been cooked as it's full of vitamins but keep it as a stock or the base for a soup. As a child in the 1950s, I was not a lover of eating cabbage but I would happily drink a cup of hot cabbage water flavoured with Marmite (yeast extract) and benefit from all those vitamins. This was Mum's idea and a hangover from her wartime experiences.

> loyally to the rationing regulations. Above all, when you are shopping, cooking or eating – remember, 'Food is a Munition of War. Don't waste it!'

You can be prosecuted for wasting food, so be careful.

A book, *Nutrition & The War* by Dr Geoffrey Bourne, published in 1942,[1] is very different from what we might read in the twenty-first century because everyone needs calories to keep warm and have enough energy. Whereas nowadays, so many people want to reduce their intake of calories, this book describes an apple as 'poor' in calories and bacon as 'very good', so you must forget about slimming diets. You need calories! This book estimates that a man lying in a warm bed, doing nothing but existing, still burns up to 2,000 calories a day. Working hard at a task, such as digging out people from a collapsed building after a bombing raid, can burn more than 5,000 calories. Simply sitting at home on a chilly day without any heating – which some do to conserve fuel – requires around 3,000 calories because shivering uses quite a bit of energy and your body must burn calories to maintain its optimum temperature. There's every chance that you'll be slimmer and fitter by the time you end your visit than you were when you arrived.

Shopping

Armed with your ration book, coupons and a few shillings and pence to spend, what can you buy?

In 1943, this is an example of the weekly rations for an adult:

3 pints of milk

¾ lb–1 lb of meat – the variation is because meat is rationed by price: quality not quantity

1 egg (or 1 packet of US dried eggs every 2 months, available from 1942)

3–4 ozs of cheese – up to 12 ozs extra is allowed for manual labourers working outside who have to take a packed lunch and a little extra for vegetarians, of whom there are very few

4 ozs in total of bacon and/or ham

2 ozs of tea – equivalent to roughly 20 tea bags and hardly anybody drinks coffee

8 ozs of sugar

2 ozs butter

2 ozs cooking fat

Beware of mishaps with your precious rations. Christine Beech recalls one of her mum's wartime cautionary tales about the time Christine's elder brother, a toddler in his highchair, reached out and grabbed the family's entire weekly butter ration and ate it all in a few mouthfuls. A butterless week must have followed but the toddler certainly made sure of his share.[2]

In addition to your rations, a system of sixteen points allocated to each adult every month will allow you to buy one can of fish or meat or 2 lbs of dried fruit or 8 lbs of split peas, all subject to availability. A tin of sardines can liven up a salad or, under the US 'Lend-Lease'

Scheme, you could try something quite new to the British menu: American tinned sausage meat, corned beef or Spam (Supply Pressed American Meat, mostly pork). People aren't sure about these but the sausage meat comes surrounded by precious fat, which is saved for frying and roasting other foods, and it tastes good. At least corned beef looks like meat but Spam – pale pink, smooth, without any texture and not much flavour – is slow to meet the customer's approval. Spam is part of an American GI's army rations and they often eat it straight from the tin but, at first sight, it just doesn't appeal to British meat-lovers. However, sliced in a sandwich, daubed with homemade chutney, I can testify to Spam being perfectly edible and definitely better than nothing.

Bread becomes a problem. The government manages to avoid rationing bread until after the war but, previously, we had relied on grain imports from Canada, especially of wheat to produce white bread. Now we have to use homegrown grain and nothing can be wasted. The result is the National Loaf, introduced in 1941, much to the disgust of customers who want their white bread as before but it's

SPAM. *New York Post*

Did You Know?

In 1942, Eleanor Roosevelt, America's First Lady, visited King George VI and his wife, Queen Elizabeth, at Buckingham Palace and she recalled: 'We were served on gold and silver plates but our bread was the same kind of war bread every other family had to eat.'[3]

no longer produced. In the twenty-first century, we happily accept wholemeal bread and we know it's a healthier option than white. But, at the time, people don't like this muddy-coloured bread. Perhaps you can buy a National Loaf with a smile and convince them that it's good for them as well as for the war effort.

Always leave plenty of time for shopping because the chances are that you'll probably have to join a queue if you want an onion from the greengrocer, liver from the butcher or that Easter treat: a couple of hot cross buns from the baker. Rationing is supposed to do away with the need to queue which was such a huge problem

Queuing. Douglas Miller Keystone Getty Images

in the Great War. However, the government quickly realises that this isn't the case and issues 'priority shopping cards' to women engaged in war work who can't afford to waste time, waiting in line, giving them the right to go to the front of the queue. But this doesn't work either because so many women are doing valuable war work, resulting in queues even of those with priority cards. And after all that queuing, if you're unlucky, just as you reach the front of the line, the commodity you are hoping to buy is sold out. Better luck next time.

Other steps are taken by the authorities to share out supplies, so that eggs, fruit, vegetables and farm produce aren't all kept in the countryside but also distributed in towns.

Growing your own

One partial solution is to grow what food you can for yourself, if you have a garden plot. 'Dig for Victory!' That's the slogan to encourage everyone with a garden, however small, an allotment or strip of spare land to grow vegetables and fruit, keep chickens or maybe a pig. Anything to provide extra food for the nation. Many beautiful London parks are dug up and allocated by the local council to people who apply for a small 'allotment' to plant and harvest produce.

If you arrive back in the autumn of 1939 and your new neighbours are busy digging up their beautiful lawn and planting all kinds of winter crops, you might do well to suggest they wait until spring because you know what's coming. The winter of 1939–1940 is going to be the coldest for fifty years with deep snow in January and hard frosts, killing off most of these early efforts at growing your own vegetables.

The government issues a whole series of leaflets to advise those taking up gardening for the first time. Leaflet No. 1 is about planting vegetables for winter as well as summer, hence all that autumn planting. But, oddly, you have to wait for Leaflet No. 20 for instructions on 'how to dig', which probably should have come first. In October 1939, a wall chart is available, showing how to do 'crop rotation' on a three-year cycle, dividing your plot into three areas. You grow peas, beans, onions and leeks the first year; root crops like potatoes, carrots and parsnips the second; and members of the cabbage family in the third year on the same area. This allows the peas and beans to improve the soil so your root crops next year grow better. Cabbages, sprouts, kale, cauliflowers, etc. shouldn't be grown in the same soil two years in succession so the disease club-root can't take hold and ruin your leafy vegetables.

Garden experts writing these leaflets and hundreds of articles in magazines are slow to credit women with the ability to do heavy work. Digging is reckoned to be a man's work while women sprinkle seeds and do light weeding. In photos and illustrations, women are often depicted wearing jaunty hats, skirts and dainty footwear. But girls know better…

A woman in Sheffield, over 70 years old, had two allotments for which she won a medal, hoping to inspire other women. In 1942, a Cornish woman harvested almost 100 lbs of onions, more than 7 hundredweight of potatoes and 1,500 leeks from her plot, plus other vegetables, despite working eight-hour days in a factory, keeping chickens, running her house and caring for two children.[4] Phew!

Marion Cashman was a small child during the war. Her father worked at the Arsenal in Woolwich so was in a reserved occupation (see Chapter 5) as well as serving in the Home Guard. The family lived at Welling in North-West Kent and suffered some near misses during the Blitz. They had a fair-sized garden and Marion's father and her grandfather grew potatoes, carrots, swedes, onions, cabbages, beetroots, lettuces, tomatoes and cress – enough to keep the whole family supplied. She remembers her grandfather showing her how to cut cabbages and lettuces above the ground, leaving the stump and roots in place so they grew a second crop of leaves. They would share

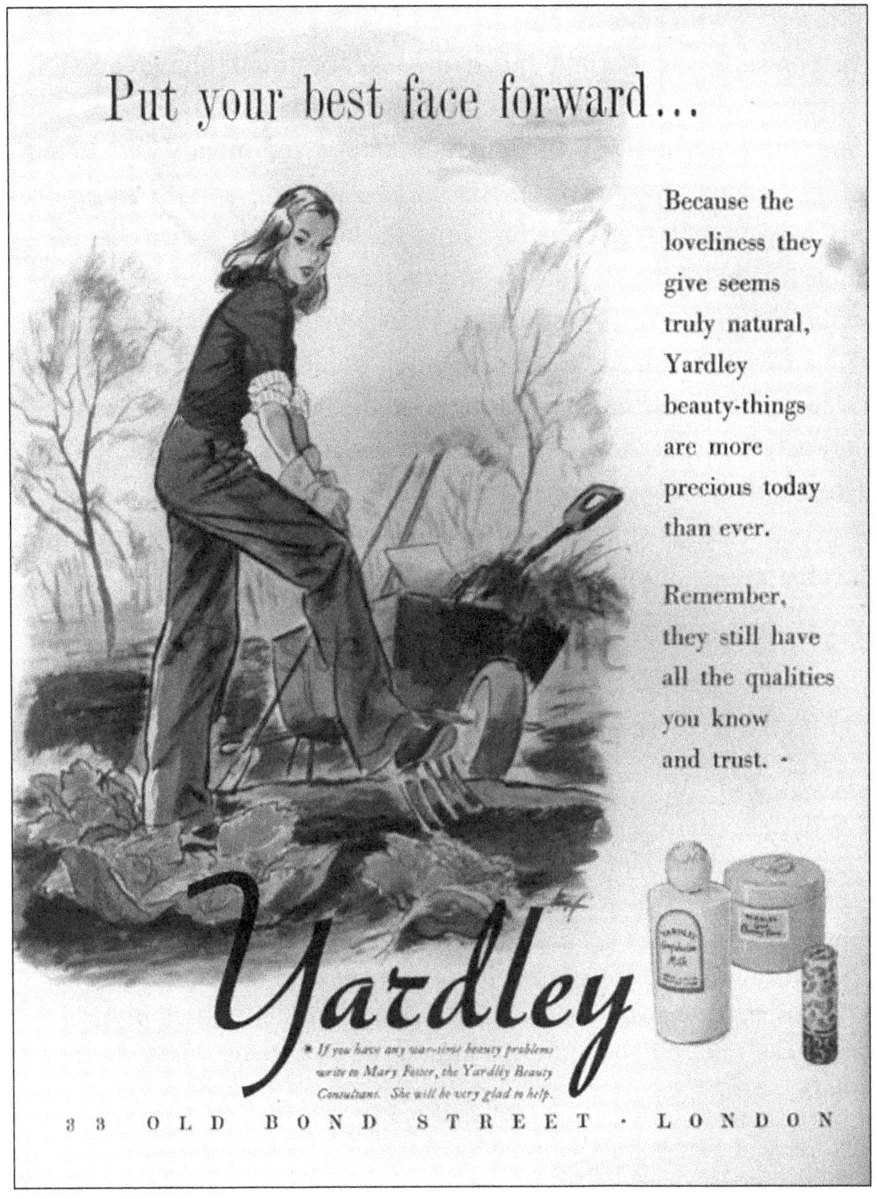

A Yardley advertisement in *Good Housekeeping* magazine

produce and exchange seedlings and cuttings with other gardeners. Little Marion 'did her bit' by helping with the weeding and singing a song to the neighbour's chickens: 'Chick, chick, chick, chick, chicken, lay a little egg for me', to encourage them to lay.[5]

Keeping chickens is encouraged. As early as December 1939, *The Gardeners' Chronicle* magazine is recommending that amateur gardeners with enough space outside should keep livestock of some kind, particularly those which can be fed mostly on kitchen scraps because food for animals will be in short supply and more expensive as the war goes on – and the magazine is correct. They suggest keeping hens, ducks – if you have a pond – geese, rabbits, goats and pigs. Amy Thomas lives in Northfleet, Kent, in a road of Victorian terraced houses without much in the way of front gardens but long, narrow gardens at the back with a communal alleyway behind. Amy was born in the house where one of her sisters still lives – one of thirteen children in two bedrooms and a box room! Let's ask her about keeping hens in her back garden and the challenges involved:

'Amy, I see you've got quite a few eggs there. How many hens do you have?'

'I have six now and a cockerel – though some of my neighbours complain about him. Now it's summer, he wakes us up, crowing before four o'clock in the morning. If there have been raids in London overnight, we don't get much sleep. But Rufus – the cock – keeps his girls happy. I used to have seven hens but one didn't lay so we had her for a special Sunday dinner on my daughter's birthday back in April. You can't be soft about these things but I liked Betty; she was quite tame.'

'I've read that you're supposed to have a permit to keep chickens. Is that true?'

'Officially, yes, but you only need to show it, if you want to buy chicken-feed and we manage without it. Maize is – or was – imported from America so it's in as short supply as decent flour for bread. We feed the hens on weeds and kitchen scraps. Our neighbours save any groundsel, chickweed, charlock, speedwell, dandelions and the like when they weed their plots and give it to us for the hens. We share our eggs around the street but we ask everyone to return the egg shells.'

'Why on earth…'

'Because the hens need the calcium in the shells to make sure the next eggs they lay aren't too thin shelled. If they are, the eggs break so easily the chicken can accidentally smash what she lays. We also feed them any suitable kitchen scraps although I give most of the potato skins to my sister, Hilda, who lives five houses farther up the road, for her rabbits. The animals live in old tea chests which our brother Wallace converted into hutches.'

'And where do you keep your chickens?'

'In a proper chicken run with a nice hen-house at the bottom of the garden. My younger son, Harold, did most of the work before he was old enough to join the navy – poor boy. [Dabs her eyes.] He won't be coming back. [Sighs.] Still, we have to carry on, don't we?'

'I'm sorry to hear that. I see you're growing vegetables too. Your cabbages look huge.'

'Yes, and the hens help with that. During the day, I let them roam and they eat the caterpillars off the plants and spread their droppings as manure at the same time. It works well. I'm also growing potatoes, beetroots, radishes and salad stuff, onions, parsnips, carrots and runner beans – the lawn never was worth the trouble. Oh, and tomatoes in the cold frame. And the cooking-apple tree, of course, and my favourite rose bush and some lupins and marigolds from before the war. A few flowers really cheer you up, don't they? Now, I have to take these eggs to the shop opposite and exchange them for a bit of extra cheese. Then I must dig up the first of our early potato crop and we'll have cheese and potato crumble for dinner with fresh lettuce.'[6]

And with the idea of cheese and potato crumble for dinner, we now need to think about cooking: methods of saving precious fuel and how to stretch the weekly rations to make filling and nutritious meals.

Poster to encourage saving kitchen scraps to feed chickens. TNA

Cooking

> The Ministry of Food asks every housewife to read, listen and watch:
>
> Read – Most newspapers and magazines are running special wartime cookery features. It is a good plan to cut out the items that interest you and keep them handy in scrapbook.
>
> Listen – Broadcasts have been arranged to give all the latest practical information about buying, preparing and cooking food. Look out for them. They tell what foods are in season and how they can be used.
>
> Watch – Simple demonstrations in cookery and meal planning are being arranged up and down the country. Ask for particulars from your local Food Office or Education Authority. Go along and take your friends.
>
> (Issued by His Majesty's Stationery Office)

The Ministry of Food deluges the public with 'Food Facts' in magazines and 'Food Flashes' at the cinema. It employs professional cooks, like Marguerite Patten – the Jamie Oliver of the day – to staff their advice centres and give demonstrations in various places, from school kitchens to the foyer at Harrods. Most important is the daily five-minute 'Kitchen Front' programme broadcast on the wireless every morning at 8.00 am, immediately after the news, which shows how vital it is and everyone is expected to be listening in. The ministry does its best to drive the message home with catchy little jingles like this:

Those who have the will to win
Cook potatoes in their skin,
Knowing that the sight of peelings
Deeply hurts Lord Woolton's feelings.

Song of Potato Pete

Potatoes new, potatoes old
Potato (in a salad) cold
Potatoes baked or mashed or
fried
Potatoes whole, potato pied
Enjoy them all, including chips
Remembering spuds don't come
in ships!

Potato Pete's Song. TNA

Lord Woolton, the Minister of Food, is quite a hero. He even has a recipe named after him which you may like to try.

Metric measurements are given but they won't appear on 1940s kitchen scales. This is the recipe for Woolton Pie to serve four people.

For the pastry you'll need:

8 ozs [225 g] wholemeal flour

2 teaspoons baking powder

3 ozs [85 g] margarine or lard

4 ozs [110 g] cold mashed potato

Pinch of salt

Milk to glaze

For the filling:

14 ozs [400 g] each of roughly chopped cauliflower; peeled and chopped parsnips, carrots and potatoes

3 spring [salad] onions

1–2 teaspoons of yeast extract

1 tablespoon of oatmeal

1 tablespoon of fresh chopped parsley [or 1 teaspoon of dried]

Salt and pepper

To make the pastry: mix together the flour, baking powder and salt in a large bowl. Add the margarine or lard and rub in with your fingertips. Add the mashed potato and bring together to form a dough, adding a splash of water if needed. Cover and set aside in a cold place for an hour – in the fridge if you have one.

Preheat the oven to 200°C [180°C for a twenty-first-century fan oven] or gas mark 6.

To make the filling: put the vegetables, yeast extract, oatmeal, salt and pepper in a large saucepan, allowing room for the oats to swell, and just cover with water. Bring to the boil and simmer for 15 minutes or until most of the water has gone and the filling has thickened. Allow to cool.

Put the filling into a pie dish and sprinkle the parsley over it. Roll out the pastry to make a lid to top the dish and brush it with milk.

Bake for 30 minutes or until golden brown.

Serve your Woolton Pie sliced with greens and gravy. Enjoy![7]

Did You Know?

Carrot cake and fruit crumbles, still popular today, are invented during rationing. Carrots are quite sweet so using them as a cake mix ingredient means you need far less precious sugar. A crumble topping on cooked fruit replaces a pie crust, saving on both flour and cooking time, saving fuel.

Eating your pie is a knife-and-fork job but for some evacuees, cutlery is something they're not used to at home – and nor are fruit, vegetables, jam or even soup. Some city children seem to exist on broken biscuits, Oxo cubes and bags of chips eaten on the doorstep. Now, as evacuees, they're expected to sit and eat at a table, something never known before. Two lads, aged 10 and 12, even try to eat soup with a knife and fork. You have to wonder what they think of some wartime favourites which, to them, must seem more foreign than sushi today.[8]

You'll probably like a sweet dish to follow your Woolton's Pie.

Marguerite Patten's recipe for Rhubarb Crumble for four people.

For the filling:

1 lb rhubarb

2 tablespoons golden syrup

For the crumble:

1½ oz margarine or lard

4 ozs plain flour

3 tablespoons sugar

A pinch of salt

To prepare the rhubarb: wipe the rhubarb stalks clean, cut off any leaf as they're poisonous! Cut the stalks into small pieces. Simmer them with the syrup until cooked and beginning to soften. Put the rhubarb in the bottom of a pie dish or individual oven-proof dishes.

To prepare the crumble:

Rub the fat into the flour, sugar and salt until it looks like fine breadcrumbs. Sprinkle the crumble over the rhubarb and bake in a moderate oven for 15–20 minutes until the crumble crisps up.[9]

The Ministry of Food's War Cookery Leaflet No. 9 is all about fuel saving in the kitchen. Overcooking food wastes fuel and destroys vitamins. Keep saucepans scrupulously clean but NOT ON THE BOTTOM as a dull surface takes up heat quicker than a shiny one. Always put a lid or a plate on top of a saucepan to keep in the heat. If you don't have a steamer, put a colander on top of a boiling pudding to cook a vegetable, putting a plate or saucepan lid on top of the colander. Shred or dice vegetables so they cook more quickly and put them in the same saucepan. Make cakes, crumbles and even pies and puddings in individual ovenproof teacups, little basins or patty tins; the smaller size means they cook quicker. Bone meat before roasting as it'll cook quicker, then boil bones to make stock or soup. Dried fruit, peas, beans and lentils will be soaked and ready to cook if you pour boiling water on them and leave them in a hay box overnight. Oatmeal can be treated this way and your porridge will be ready to eat for breakfast. Plan ahead: never use the oven to cook a single dish and have one big baking session each week. And finally, can you cooperate with your neighbour so you take turns cooking meals for each other so only one oven is used each day but both families get hot meals.

You can make your own portable hay box. It's basically a box which is insulated on the bottom and the sides with hay, newspaper or whatever is to hand. Bring your soup, stew, casserole or porridge to the boil then put the saucepan into the hay box lined with hay. Put the lid on the pan and pack hay all around it before putting another thick layer of insulation on top. Close the box and leave it alone

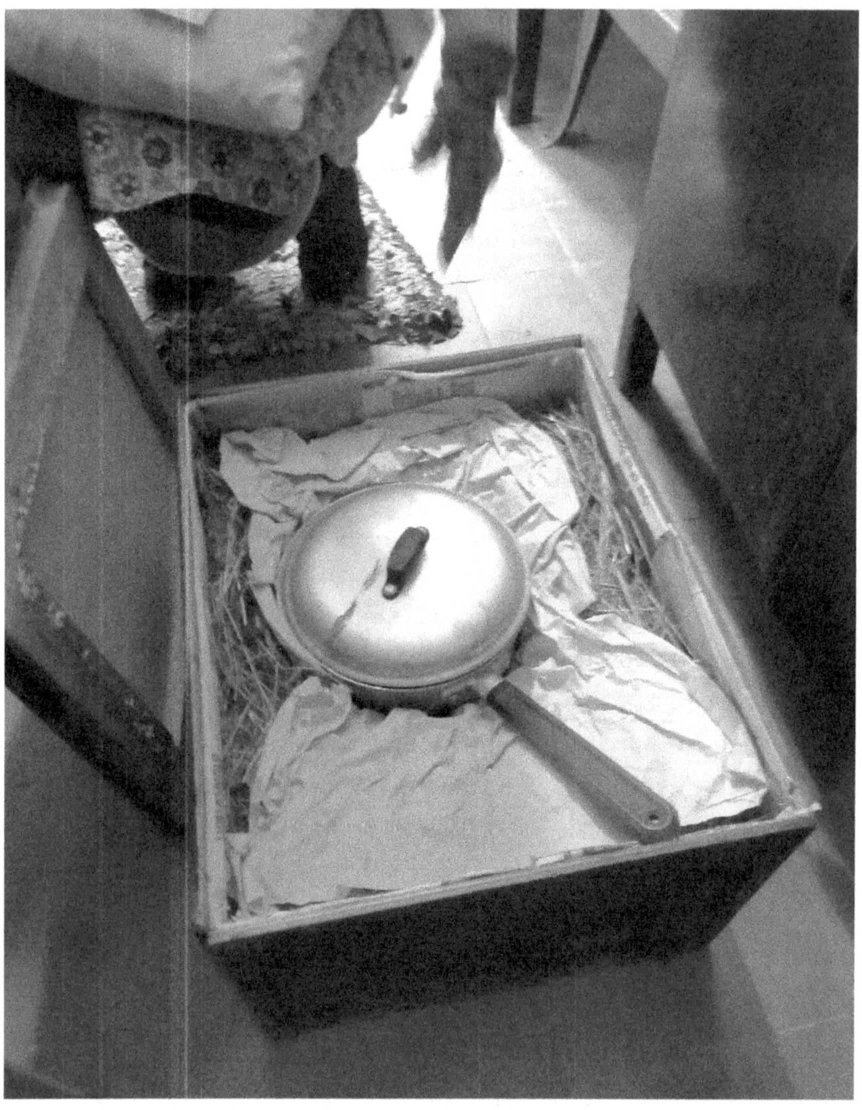

A hay box. World War II House, Sittingbourne, GRM

until morning. If you want to make a hay box from a spare gas-mask carrier, full instructions will be sent to you if you write to the Ministry of Food. They say, 'It's very simple and will make a useful Christmas present.'

A foodstuff which is new to everyone is powdered egg, another US import which takes getting used to. It reconstitutes as one tablespoon of powdered egg to two tablespoons of water equals one egg. Some people hate it but Mum said the family was sad when powdered egg was no longer available after the war as it made the best scrambled eggs and omelettes.

Here is the recipe for Sadie's Cheese Omelette.

4 dried eggs reconstituted from 4 level tablespoons of egg powder mixed with 8 tablespoons of water

Salt and pepper

2 ozs [50 g] grated cheese

½ oz margarine

Add seasoning to the reconstituted egg. Heat the margarine in a pan, pour in the egg and work the mixture with a fork. As the egg begins to set, sprinkle in the grated cheese and cook for another minute. Fold the omelette and serve with watercress or other fresh green leafy vegetable.[10]

Eating away from home

With the war effort underway, it would waste precious manufacturing time if workers have to leave the factory and go home for their midday meal, as they did before the war. Works canteens are set up to feed the workforce and save time. Eating in the canteen may not be *haute cuisine* but you'll be eating with your mates and colleagues and – importantly – you don't need your ration book, so you also save your precious rations.

If you can afford it, eating in cafés, hotels and restaurants also saves your rations, which seems unfair to those who can't spare the cash for such luxuries. In 1943, the government prohibits hotels and restaurants from charging more than five shillings per head per meal and allows no more than three courses. But even this means many can't afford to eat out and stretch their rations.

Cheaper alternatives are the government-run British Restaurants, often set up in abandoned restaurants, village halls and evacuated schools: any places with catering facilities. Like the works canteens, food is basic but nutritious and doesn't require points or coupons. Some people hate them, seeing the meals as cheap charity handouts but, in Sheffield in Yorkshire, the City Council runs Civil Restaurants and these are so successful that in 1947, the council intends to continue the scheme, despite protests from private restaurant owners.

A famous chain of less expensive cafés is the Lyons Corner Houses. These become popular places to meet and eat with friends. Many Lyons cafés are in London and somehow manage to reopen and feed customers despite suffering bomb damage. Where bomb damage is too severe, you'll probably find the WVS or the Salvation Army setting up 'pop-up' canteens in any building still standing to serve the rescue workers and those made homeless.

For evacuees and school children there is the prospect of school dinners. With many mothers now involved in war work, it's easier if the children eat together at midday instead of going home. Before the war, in 1934, realising many youngsters were malnourished, the School Medical Officer for Glossop designed a free school meal to supply all the components of a healthy diet. It becomes known as the Glossop Health Sandwich and, because it requires no cooking, it's useful in saving fuel and providing a meal where cooking isn't possible. Here's the recipe for the Glossop Health Sandwich:

1 pint of milk and 1 orange, when obtainable

If no fruit then ¼ oz of chopped parsley to be included in the sandwich filling

3 ozs wholemeal bread

¾ oz butter or vitaminised margarine

¾ oz of salad: mustard-and-cress or water cress or lettuce or tomato or grated carrot

1½ ozs of cheese or tinned salmon or herring or sardine or liver paste

A pinch of dried brewer's yeast

Some schools don't have kitchens and, with the number of pupils swollen by evacuees, lacking the space for mass-dining, church halls and village halls may have to be pressed into emergency catering. In her village of Shere in Surrey, Connie Miles helps out in the village hall at school dinnertime. On Tuesday, 7 July 1942, she notes:

> Watched the pandemonium in the children's kitchen from my seat at the money table. Grown-ups flying about in the greatest haste; children holding out plates in a desperate manner, as if to say, 'Don't forget me.' I grow very severe these days and insist on 'please' before I take their orders.[11]

Now you know about the food available, how can you keep healthy and safe? The next chapter will help you.

Chapter 4

How Can I Keep Healthy and Safe?

Believe it or not, one incidental result of rationing and the re-organising of essential food supplies across the country is an actual improvement in the general health of everybody. In 1939, before rationing began, more than half the people of Britain were suffering some level of malnutrition, most often vitamin deficiency in some form. Lack of vitamin D and sunshine led to growing children suffering from rickets, resulting in bow-legs. Lack of vitamin C from fresh fruit and vegetables could cause symptoms of scurvy, beginning with fatigue and bruising easily and, if it continued, gum disease, poor healing of wounds and depression.

Getting your vitamins

Although, throughout rationing, the average daily intake of calories remains around 3,000, as it was before the war, there are major changes to the diet because the discrepancies between the diets of the better off and the poorer people are greatly reduced. Lord Woolton's National Milk Scheme concentrates the limited supplies on children and priority adults, including pregnant women, mothers who are breastfeeding, the elderly and infirm. By 1943, the consumption of milk per head has trebled in some deprived areas. The Vitamin Welfare Scheme for children is introduced in December 1941 to supply them with cod liver oil – very good for them but horrible – and later on, when available, orange juice. Pregnant women also receive iron pills to prevent anaemia.

War Cookery Leaflet No. 10 is headed 'Your Children's Food in Wartime':

> You want your children to be healthy and happy, of course; and to grow up strong and sturdy. Do you know that all that depends very largely upon the food you give them now and the food habits you help them to form? By following the few simple rules given in this leaflet, you can do much to make sure that your children build sound constitutions and healthy, active bodies.

I'm not suggesting you, as a visitor, will take young children back in time with you but, with so many evacuees and displaced families due to the bombing, it's as well if you understand what the youngsters need and are entitled to have. The leaflet stresses that the 'priority' milk for the children MUST NOT be given to the grown-ups. Every child over 2 years is entitled to the full cheese and meat ration – again, the leaflet states, 'DO NOT give grown-ups the children's meat' – and those under 5 should have the full egg ration, which decreases once they're 6. Liver and oily fish are recommended alternatives to make up for the reduction in eggs for older children.

Green vegetables and/or root vegetables are a must, the latter sprinkled with chopped parsley and mashed, if being served to toddlers. However, the leaflet advises: 'Do not force children to eat a particular food. This tends to create a permanent dislike for it.' This can cause difficulties as school dinner ladies, as I remember, used

Did You Know?

Fish is never rationed but with so many fishermen joining the navy and the dangers from German U-Boats in the fishing grounds, fish is scarce and an unreliable food source. It's also expensive. Later in the war, whale meat and 'snoek' are unpopular alternatives to the old favourites: cod, haddock and herring. But tinned fish, such as sardines, salmon, pilchards and herrings are available, if you have enough coupons.

to make you sit with your plate of soggy cabbage going cold and there was no dessert or playtime until the plate was empty. I wish they'd read Leaflet No. 10. Even at home, you were expected to eat everything put in front of you: 'waste not, want not' was the rule in our house long after rationing ended.

Fruit should be served to children every day, as the leaflet advises, but this may not be possible. As alternatives, blackcurrant syrup or puree can be had at the Food Office or from the Welfare Clinic. Even better, rosehip syrup – full of vitamin C – is available from the chemist so adults can benefit from this immunity booster and cold remedy too. Or, make your own rosehip syrup, jam or jelly; recipes available from the Food Office or Food Advice Centre. By 1943, 500 tons of rosehips are being gathered from the hedgerows each year, enough to make 2,500,000 bottles of syrup, saving the import of 25,000,000 oranges. Children are paid 3d per 1 lb for the hips by the government for the commercial manufacturers of rosehip syrup.

Free fare from the hedgerows

In 1943 (one source gives 1945), the Ministry of Food issued a leaflet, 'Hedgerow Harvest', instructing 'townies' how to gather wild fruits, nuts and mushrooms from the countryside – food for free, just so long as you know your sloes from your deadly nightshade, your edible mushrooms from the lethal toadstools.

The leaflet gives this recipe for making your own rosehip syrup.

Ingredients:

2 lbs [900 g] of washed wild rosehips

1¼ lbs [560 g] of preserving sugar

3 pints [1.7 litres] of water + a further 1½ pints [852 ml]

Method:

Bring the water to the boil in a saucepan. Mince the rosehips in a course mincer [a hand-cranked food processor] and put them immediately into the boiling water. Bring back to the boil and then set aside to cool for 15 minutes. Pour the rosehips and water into a flannel or linen jelly bag and allow to drip into a basin until most of the liquid has come through.

Return the residue left in the jelly bag to the saucepan, add 1½ pints [852 ml] of boiling water, stir and allow to stand for 10 minutes. Pour this back into the jelly bag and allow to drip.

To make sure all the sharp hairs are removed put back the first half cupful of liquid and allow to drip through again.

Put the mixed juice into a clean saucepan and boil down until the juice measures about 1½ pints [852 ml], then add 1¼ lbs [560 g] of sugar and boil for a further 5 minutes.

Pour into hot sterile bottles and seal at once.

Hints:

If you are using corks, these should have been boiled for an hour just previously and, after inserting them in the neck of the bottles, seal them with melted paraffin wax. It's best to use small bottles as the syrup will not keep for more than a week or two once the bottle is opened. Store in a dark cupboard and use your rosehip syrup as a flavouring for milk puddings, ice-cream or almost any sweet, or diluted as a drink.[1]

Top Tip

Even if you grow your own fruit, making jams and preserves from it is tricky as sugar is rationed and you aren't likely to be able to get enough sugar, unless you have some food item you can swap with someone else for their sugar. Many people start saving up their sugar rations in early summer to help with jam-making time. (Some years, during the summer, the Ministry of Food is able to double the sugar rations to encourage home preserving.)

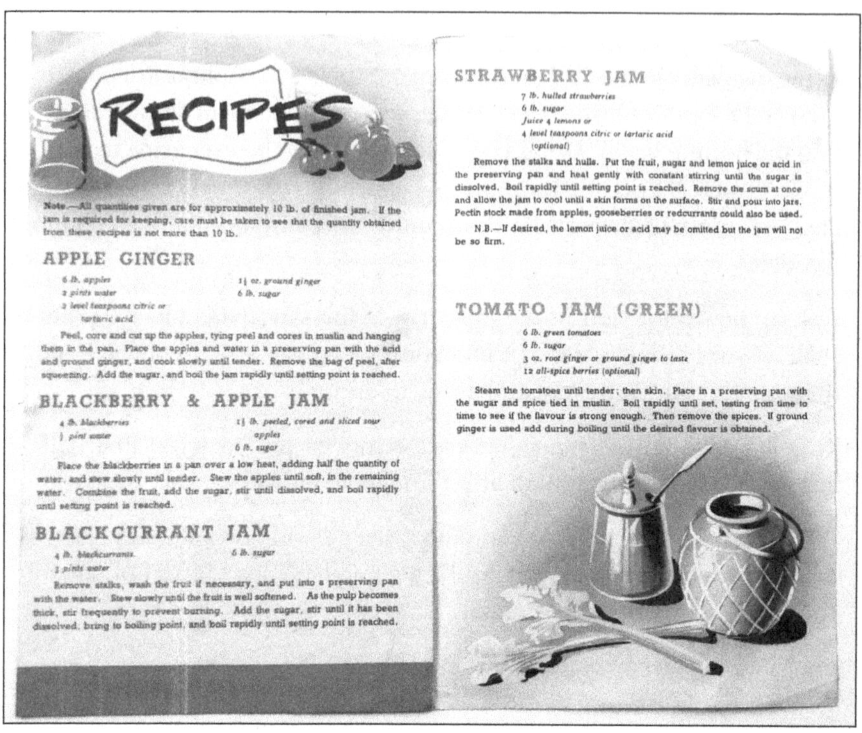

RECIPES

Note.—All quantities given are for approximately 10 lb. of finished jam. If the jam is required for keeping, care must be taken to see that the quantity obtained from these recipes is not more than 10 lb.

APPLE GINGER

6 lb. apples
2 pints water
2 level teaspoons citric or tartaric acid
1½ oz. ground ginger
6 lb. sugar

Peel, core and cut up the apples, tying peel and cores in muslin and hanging them in the pan. Place the apples and water in a preserving pan with the acid and ground ginger, and cook slowly until tender. Remove the bag of peel, after squeezing. Add the sugar, and boil the jam rapidly until setting point is reached.

BLACKBERRY & APPLE JAM

4 lb. blackberries
½ pint water
1½ lb. peeled, cored and sliced sour apples
6 lb. sugar

Place the blackberries in a pan over a low heat, adding half the quantity of water, and stew slowly until tender. Stew the apples until soft, in the remaining water. Combine the fruit, add the sugar, stir until dissolved, and boil rapidly until setting point is reached.

BLACKCURRANT JAM

4 lb. blackcurrants
3 pints water
6 lb. sugar

Remove stalks, wash the fruit if necessary, and put into a preserving pan with the water. Stew slowly until the fruit is well softened. As the pulp becomes thick, stir frequently to prevent burning. Add the sugar, stir until it has been dissolved, bring to boiling point, and boil rapidly until setting point is reached.

STRAWBERRY JAM

7 lb. hulled strawberries
6 lb. sugar
Juice 4 lemons or
4 level teaspoons citric or tartaric acid (optional)

Remove the stalks and hulls. Put the fruit, sugar and lemon juice or acid in the preserving pan and heat gently with constant stirring until the sugar is dissolved. Boil rapidly until setting point is reached. Remove the scum at once and allow the jam to cool until a skin forms on the surface. Stir and pour into jars. Pectin stock made from apples, gooseberries or redcurrants could also be used.

N.B.—If desired, the lemon juice or acid may be omitted but the jam will not be so firm.

TOMATO JAM (GREEN)

6 lb. green tomatoes
6 lb. sugar
3 oz. root ginger or ground ginger to taste
12 all-spice berries (optional)

Steam the tomatoes until tender; then skin. Place in a preserving pan with the sugar and spice tied in muslin. Boil rapidly until set, testing from time to time to see if the flavour is strong enough. Then remove the spices. If ground ginger is used add during boiling until the desired flavour is obtained.

Ministry of Food Leaflet No. 28, 'Jam Making'

Boy Scouts, Girl Guides, Women's Institutes and school children are in action every summer and autumn, doing their bit for the war effort as the government sets up seventy County Herb Committees and 250 drying centres across Britain, overseen by the Vegetable Drugs Committee. Apart from rosehips, deadly nightshade is collected to produce a drug used in eye surgery. Foxgloves for a drug which helps irregular heartbeat. Opium poppies give morphine and many other

Did You Know?

During the Great War, children had collected horse chestnuts (conkers), not for use in drug manufacture – and this was top secret at the time – but for the production of explosives! In 1917, 3,000 tons of conkers were collected.[2]

herbs are gathered for the pharmaceutical industry. Also, to help the war effort, by 1943, sugar-coating on pills is stopped, so you may need a dash of jam to take away the horrible taste of any medication.

Staying healthy

Lord Woolton wants everyone to be fit and in good spirits and in this chatty quotation from early in 1940 he tells you how to do this:

> You want to get through your work and difficulties with the same spirit you expect of the Forces in action. Well, thanks to government planning, the foods that will feed you and your family to the pitch of fighting fitness are right at your hand. They have been deliberately chosen to that purpose. To release ships and seamen on the fighting fronts, you, on the Kitchen Front, have the job of using these foods to the greatest advantage. Here's how to do it –
>
> FIRST: Your rations and allowances. These are the foundation of your fighting diet. Take your full share of them always.
>
> NEXT: Vegetables. These provide many of the vitamins so essential for good health and buoyant vitality.
>
> THIRD: Unrefined or wholegrain foods – flour, oats, etc. These also supply valuable health factors and, of course, add bulk to build up satisfying meals.
>
> Spread your rations and allowances so that you get part of each of them every day, making sure that each member of your family gets their proper share.

A government health booklet, *How to Keep Well in Wartime*, is published in 1943, price 3d. Its first section deals with 'regular living

'How to Keep Well in Wartime' leaflet from His Majesty's Stationery Office, 1943

habits', primarily the importance of your early-morning visit to the WC (the 'water closet', the loo, toilet, lavatory, bathroom or whatever you call it). This seems to be a bit of an obsession at the time and constipation can be cured, so it says – you guessed it – by eating more vegetables.

Getting enough sleep is No. 2 on the list and at least eight hours a night is essential or you'll feel run down. It doesn't mention how to manage this with constant air raids every night, though it suggests using ear plugs or cotton wool to keep out noise but then you won't hear the air-raid siren either.

Getting your share of air and sunshine is No. 3, with tips on how to ventilate a room *and* comply with blackout regulations (see Chapter 1 and below). Avoid stuffy and overheated rooms and take every opportunity to 'give your skin a good airing' outside. I don't think it means nude sunbathing, but feeling the sunshine and fresh air is invigorating. This comes with the warning to avoid too much sun but the use of sunscreen isn't mentioned as the harmful effect of UV rays isn't understood. Perhaps you can advise your friends.

Keeping mind and body active is covered in section No. 4. It begins by suggesting a visit to the seaside to go swimming or use the local swimming baths. But there's a problem here: public access to beaches is forbidden as they're draped in barbed wire and sometimes mined to prevent the enemy landing and both public and private pools are closed because the fuel can't be wasted heating so much water.

Exercise is essential but you also need to relax by walking, cycling, digging or rowing a boat. 'Advice to the Fat' – there's no such thing as political correctness in the 1940s – is to begin exercising gradually. 'Advice to those Underweight' is simply to eat their full ration. Being too 'lean' makes you prone to contracting TB (tuberculosis).

Choosing the right food is dealt with in section No. 5 – a long piece which we've covered above and in Chapter 3. Section 6 is about being moderate in all things. It begins with 'Are we smoking too much?' You and I know smoking is bad for your health in every way but nobody understands its links to cancer during the war. Incredibly, it quotes King James I who, way back at the beginning of the seventeenth century, disapproved of tobacco smoking, saying 'it is hateful to the nose… dangerous to the lungs… the black stinking fume thereof…' The author of the leaflet notes that this is 'laying it on a bit thick' but you know better.

The leaflet also advises moderation in drinking tea, coffee and alcohol and to be responsible about sex and discusses the problems of venereal diseases.

Section no. 7 is 'A Word to Those Who Worry' which, in wartime, must surely be everybody. You may expect this to be about dealing with stress – as I did – but it's more psychological and emotional. It says:

> Some people, as you can observe, hate any kind of authority, whether it is in the shape of a person, an institution, the Government, the' ruling class'. Fortunately, for the moment, Hitler, Mussolini [the Italian dictator and Hitler's ally] and Nazism are useful and, incidentally, 'reasonable' targets for this kind of hatred.

So the message here is to be patient, tolerant and tactful to everyone in order to achieve happiness. Save your hatred for the enemy.

This section then goes on to talk about attitudes towards children and here it's more enlightened: give a child a sense of security by not being over-anxious yourself. Don't spoil him but encourage

Top Tip

However, a word of warning: in Ration Book Britain, just about every adult smokes. Public places and public transport are wreathed in a blue haze of tobacco smoke, so passive smoking is just about impossible to avoid, I'm afraid.

him. A happy child is a healthy child. Reason with a child rather than dictate to him: 'Do it because I tell you to' is not good enough. It takes time but reasoning patiently, explaining why the child should do something, is for the best.

Girls only

Women's personal hygiene isn't mentioned in the leaflet, being a taboo subject, but by 1941 there is a shortage of sanitary towels (pads) due to British factories focusing production on items required by the war effort. However, the shortage is so great that many women don't report to work on days when towels are needed. The problem becomes so serious that the government decides to purchase more from abroad. By 1942, the Association of Sanitary Towel Manufacturers is formed to assist in British production and distribution.

A survey is conducted in 1942 by women asking others from all backgrounds about how they cope with their periods or on 'certain days', as an advert coyly phrases it in the *Home Companion* magazine, dated 6 January 1940. Some women make their own towels from soft, absorbent rags – apparently the shirts of German prisoners-of-war officers make excellent towels and come complete with little swastika designs: the perfect way to insult the enemy. Others buy them from drapers' shops or chemists but there's a lot of embarrassment about having to ask a male assistant for them – in the days before self-service – even though sanitary products are sold in discreet, plain packaging without anything to denote what they are. The results of the survey remain secret, for government eyes only, until 1972.

Back to the leaflet on health: Sections Nos. 8 and 9 are about fighting disease by hygiene and preventing germs from spreading. Hygiene, apparently, is about avoiding catching head lice, body lice and the mites which cause scabies or 'the itch'. You can do this by having a bath or a thorough all-over wash once a week, including washing your hair. The same applies to children. Unfortunately, we

Did You Know?

My mum's World War II hero – so she told me – was Lord Nuffield because he paid for all the sanitary towels needed by women in the services throughout the war. The soft white towels were known as 'bunnies'. To be fair to the guys, he also supplied the Royal Navy with free condoms. What an incredibly worthwhile but unsung contribution to the war effort![3]

know that head lice prefer clean hair, so this may not work. Special 'nit' shampoos are likely to be in short supply but, in the twenty-first century, some genius has invented nit-combs and hair-ties impregnated with some anti-louse chemical. Maybe you could take a few with you on your journey back in time as I'm sure they'll be much appreciated.

Preventing the spread of germs covers vaccinations against typhoid, whooping cough and diphtheria. Today, children are also protected from polio, measles, mumps and rubella but these vaccines don't exist yet, so make sure you're covered before you go because, until the National Health Service is set up in July 1948, medical care will be expensive. The other preventive is to use a handkerchief when you cough or sneeze to avoid sharing your germs with others. Tissues aren't around yet and used hankies should be boiled to kill the nasties. The Ministry of Health reckons that the number of hours of work lost from the war effort due to workers taking time off with colds and flu equals the loss of production of 3,500 tanks, 1,000 bombers and 1,000,000 rifles!

The leaflet concludes with No. 10 about helping yourself to be well: 'To live, to love, to laugh, to labour to the fullness of your capacity, get fit and keep fit.' It ends with this statement: 'And just how fit you can become you probably haven't yet found out.'

So that covers how to stay healthy but, as we in the twenty-first century can't fail to be aware, alongside health is the issue of safety.

Keeping safe

Obviously, life is hazardous and even more so in wartime with bombs dropping, vehicles driving through darkened streets with virtually no headlights, broken gas mains, incendiaries and bomb craters. But the government began setting up safety measures before the war started and, as with so many other matters, the public is deluged with leaflets and information on safety.

On 4 September 1939, the day after war is declared, every household receives a fold-out leaflet, 'War Emergency – Information and Instructions'. The front cover bears the royal coat of arms, as if it has come from King George VI himself, with the words:

> Read this leaflet carefully and make sure that you and all other responsible persons in your house understand its contents.
>
> Pay no attention to rumours. Official news will be given in the papers and over the wireless.
>
> Listen carefully to all broadcast instructions and be ready to note them down.

The War Emergency Leaflet tells you to carry with you always a card, envelope or label with your full name and address clearly written on it. For children, this should be sewn onto their clothes. However, from 29 September, the government issues proper National Registration Identity Cards to everyone and this continues until 1952. The reason is so lost children, those injured or killed in an air raid can be identified, their families informed and reunited with their loved ones.

You must carry your card AT ALL TIMES – brown ones for adults but blue ones after 1943, and brown ones throughout for children under 16. The card has your full name and address with space for any updates if you're evacuated, bombed out or move because of your work. Your National Registration Number appears in the

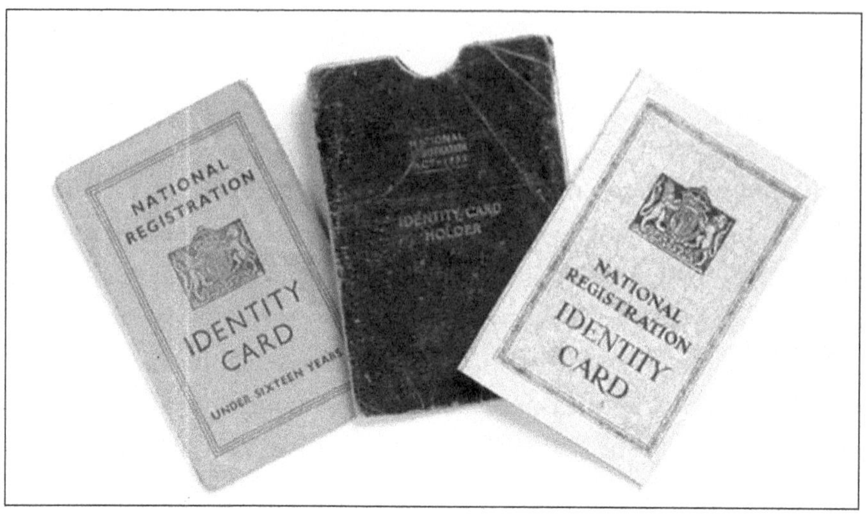

ID cards. Object Lessons

top right-hand corner and the card must be stamped by your local Registration Office to validate it once you've signed it on the back. For children, their parent or guardian has to sign and is responsible for keeping the youngster's card safe and showing it, if required.

If you work for the government, you'll be issued with a green ID card which will also have your photograph, so foreign agents can't steal your card and access government offices. If you get a job in a munitions factory, making anything from rivets for shipbuilding to high explosives, your place of work will also give you a permit, which you'll have to show at the gate. Again, this is to keep out anyone who might sabotage the place or spy on the war effort.

Attack from above

The 'War Emergency Leaflet' must have been written before the government had completely thought through its contingency plans because under 'Air Raid Warnings', it mentions the possibility of poison gas attacks but not a word about gas masks. I suppose the idea of issuing civilians – even babies and children under 5 – with a personal gas mask comes later but, within weeks of war being declared, everybody has a General Civilian Respirator, size small, medium, large and, later, extra-large, with a 'Mickey Mouse' version in bright red and blue for young children. Babies are supplied with 'hoods' which go over their head and arms with a drawstring around the waist and bellows attached which have to be pumped about forty times a minute. Your mask comes in a cardboard carton printed with instructions for use, how to put it on and keep it in a good condition.

In the Great War, gas attacks were a major feature of trench warfare and it is feared by the government that gas will be used against the

> **Top Tip**
>
> To stop the visor of your mask steaming up, smear it with soap and then polish it off.

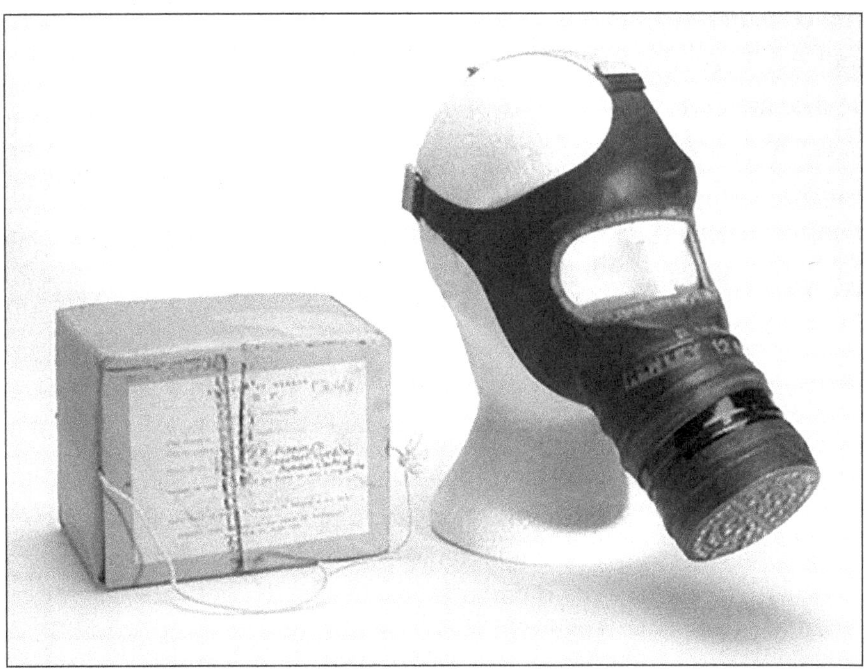

A gas mask with its box. Object Lessons

civilian population in the next. 'Take your gas mask everywhere', says the poster slogan. Fortunately, we know that gas attacks don't happen but you should still carry your mask because you could be in trouble if you haven't got it with you and some public venues, such as cinemas and dance halls, may refuse to let you in without that cardboard box hanging from your shoulder. Perhaps you can carry your lunch in it instead as a lot of people do. In fact, after a few months, less than a quarter of the population has their mask with them at all times.

As I've mentioned cinemas and dance halls, the 'War Emergency Leaflet' states that such places of entertainment will be closed until further notice. This does happen but, realising that an hour or two of fun, amusement and enjoyment boosts morale, the government allows many of them to reopen.

Trenches were burrowed into parks, gas masks were handed out like sweeties and air-raid shelters mushroomed overnight, but the conversation about what war really meant was still missing. Abject horror remained the older generation's silent burden. They had not shared their pain and now, their children, optimistic and young, were looking forward.[4]

The gas attacks, dreaded by those who remembered the Great War, never materialise but air raids certainly do. As soon as you arrive in Ration Book Britain, if it's between 1940 and 1945, you'll need to find out where the local air-raid shelters are as soon as possible, so let's ask someone who is sure to know:

'Excuse me, sir, I see you wear an ARP arm band. Can you tell me, please, what I should do if there's an air raid? I'm new here...'

'Ah, in which case, madam, I need to know your name and address. May I see your ID card, please? Oh, so you're staying with old George and Emily Burgess. Nice couple, though he's quite deaf. Sleeps through the air-raid siren, if Mrs B doesn't wake him up. He got gassed in the last lot, you know. Anyway, I'm the warden for this street, so you'll often see me around. The name's Thomas Wright: ARP Warden at your service but you can call me Tom. I live in the house on the corner.'

'What does an ARP Warden do?'

'Like it says: we deal with Air Raid Precautions, especially making sure every house is properly blacked-out after dark. I signed up for the job on the first day, back in September '39, because, at 43, I'm a couple of years too old to be called up. I get paid £3 a week as a full-time warden, though my cousin only gets £2 for the same job, being a woman. But most are part-time volunteers, like my sister. She's a secretary all day but drives an ambulance when needed. My dad serves as a Fire Watcher, so it's quite a family business, this ARP lark.'

'I see…'

'Can you believe it, though: some people didn't like us to start with; thought we were nosy, bossing them around, telling them they needed thicker curtains and to turn the light off before they opened the front door, things like that. But, since the Blitz began, now we're really appreciated because we do a lot more than that. I'm a qualified First Aider and my son John is a Boy Scout who acts as a runner, carrying messages when the telephone lines are down, keeping HQ up to date with what's happening so they can send fire engines, ambulances or whatever's needed to wherever. Last week, I was in charge of evacuating people when a bomb came down on those allotments over there but didn't explode. Got the army lads in to deal with it but it turned out to be a dud, luckily. Never could've exploded. Not like Jerry to make a mistake, is it? Except, of course, for his biggest mistake in taking us on. God Save the King. Stiff upper lip and all that, eh?'

'But can you tell me what to do, if there's an air raid, please?'

'Oh, yes, well, if the siren goes and you're at home, the Burgesses have an Anderson shelter in the garden, so you can go there until the siren goes again, meaning "all clear". If I sound my rattle, it means there's gas, put your mask on immediately and keep it on until I ring my bell to tell you the gas is gone. If you're near the railway station, there's a public shelter between the Red Lion Pub and the Railway Hotel. That's a good shelter: quite comfortable and the hotel staff make tea and sandwiches down there. The shelter in the High Street, next to Woolworth's, tends to flood in wet weather so it's not so cosy but it's better than nothing and doesn't get so crowded because of the damp.'

> 'What do you do, Tom, to keep safe in an air raid?'
>
> 'Me? Well, what can I do? I say my prayers and hope for the best, that's what. Oh, beg pardon, madam, but I see a light showing under that doorway now it's getting dark. Must dash. Duty calls.'
>
> 'Thank you, Tom, and good luck tonight, if the bombs fall…'[5]

It's the ARP Warden's job to know who lives where, which houses have their own shelter and who is likely to use the local public ones. They wear dark blue overalls with an arm band and a black helmet with a white 'W'. Chief Wardens have a white helmet with black lettering, so you'll know who's in charge. Later in the war, all ARP Wardens are issued with blue serge battledress. At the peak of the

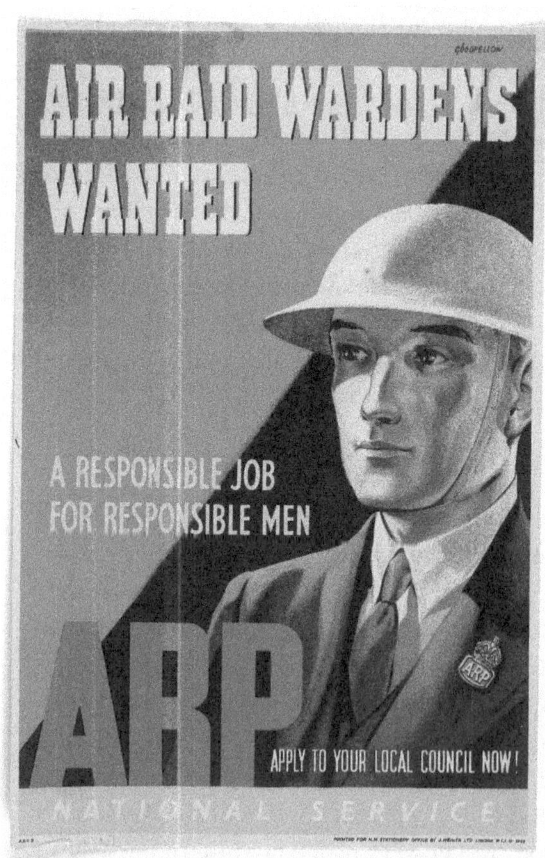

ARP poster wanting volunteers but, note, it wants men, rather than women. Wikicommons

> **Did You Know?**
>
> Miss Charity Bicks was awarded the George Medal for her bravery in 1941, working as a dispatch rider with the ARP, carrying messages on her bicycle during air raids. She was aged only 14, the youngest ever recipient of this prestigious medal.

Blitz, there are more than 130,000 full-time wardens and, despite the advertising poster's obvious bias, almost 20,000 are women. Almost a quarter of ARP unpaid volunteers are women. It's a dangerous job and almost 7,000 ARP wardens are killed during the Second World War and others win medals for their bravery.

Air-raid shelters

As the fictitious warden, Tom Wright, says above, some families have their own shelters. The Anderson shelter which he mentions goes on sale in October 1939. They're free to households which earn less than £250 a year but cost £7–£10, depending on size, for those who earn more than that, but you have to have a garden to put it in. And it's hard work because you need to dig down five or six feet (up to 2 metres) as the shelter must be partially submerged, then soil and turf are piled on top. The depth can mean that the floor is often awash with water but the space above the shelter can be planted up with vegetables. People make their Andersons as cosy as possible with chairs, bunk beds, blankets and cushions. Candles and a camping stove to brew tea, or a thermos flask, sandwiches, a pack of cards, books and board games can help pass the time. But since air raids often happen at night, most people try to get some sleep. This isn't easy with bombs dropping and the 'ack-ack' of anti-aircraft guns rattling the corrugated galvanised steel sheets which make up the shelter. They're cold and draughty, too, and prone to condensation and the 'facilities' will be a bucket in the corner.

An alternative is the Morrison Shelter, designed for use indoors for those without a garden. They come in kit form, either free or costing £7, for those better off. A Morrison is warmer and drier but you can only sit or lie down in it as it's just four feet high. About the size of a double bed, it has a solid steel top plate, a metal base with a mattress floor and wire mesh sides all round.

A more comfortable shelter for those with larger houses is to organise a 'Refuge Room', usually a basement or cellar, which you bomb-proof and gas-proof yourself – instruction pamphlet supplied. As a last resort, especially for the children, many poorer homes have 'the cupboard under the stairs', which can save lives in anything other than a direct hit.

Public shelters are provided so make sure you know where these are. If you work in a factory or commercial office with more than fifty employees, by law the employers must provide a shelter on site for everyone. Some community shelters are quite sophisticated with medical centres, toilets, food and drink laid on and even with impromptu entertainment to keep up morale.

Most famously, London Underground tube stations are used as communal shelters but, surprisingly, at first, the government refuses

Top Tip

Official *Good Night!* advice posters recommend that before going to bed, you make sure all windows and interior doors are open. It doesn't say why but probably to reduce blast damage and to make a quick escape possible. Also, to have buckets of water handy in case of fire and buckets of sand to smother incendiary bombs which can explode if you pour water on them. Keep your gas mask, torch and clothes laid ready in case you have to rush to the shelter. Although not mentioned on the *Good Night!* poster, most people have a good stout bag containing the household's important documents, such as ration books, ID cards, medical insurance card, etc., ready for any emergency.

A London Underground station being used as an air-raid shelter. Bill Brandt Collection, IWM

to allow this. When the Blitz begins in earnest on 7 September 1940, there are calls for the government to change its mind but no luck. Those MPs who object insist that the lack of mass toilet facilities will make the stations unhygienic and insanitary, that there is the huge risk of people falling onto the electrified rails and they worry that some people might take up residence permanently, disrupting commuter services.

However, on the night of 19 September, the bombing is continuous and unrelenting. Local shelters are overcrowded and some destroyed and, with no other places to seek safety, Londoners flock to shelter in the Underground stations. On 21 September, the government is forced to do a 'U-turn' and officially permit what is already happening. Seventy-nine stations are fitted out with bunkbeds for 22,000 people, the power to live rails is turned off at night, first aid and chemical toilet facilities are provided. Not long after, 124 canteens open throughout the Underground network.

Hopefully, you now have the best chance of staying healthy and keeping safe in these dangerous times, but what can you do to earn a living? The next chapter looks at what sort of jobs might suit you.

Did You Know?

In Kent, south-east of London, Chislehurst Caves, a series of prehistoric chalk and flint mines, was turned into an air-raid shelter for up to 15,000 Londoners with special trains laid on each evening and morning to transport the city-dwellers. The caves had electric lighting and included a chapel, a hospital and concerts were held.[6]

Chapter 5

What Jobs Could I Do?

On the day Britain declares war on Germany, 3 September 1939, Parliament immediately passes the National Service (Armed Forces) Act, imposing conscription on all males aged between 18 and 41 who have to register for service. Those medically unfit are exempted, as are others in key industries and jobs such as mining, farming, medicine, baking, plumbing, engineering and the clergy.

Surprisingly, the police and fire-fighters are not considered to be in 'reserved' occupations and since older members of both forces are often 'reservists' – in that they have previously served in the army or navy – and younger members are generally fit, healthy types, these men are among the first to be 'called up'. In the police, numbers are made up by recruiting reserve policemen, special constables and more women officers. In 1944, there are 43,000 regular police officers, 17,000 War Reserve Police and Special Constables and 385 women police. The Fire Brigade, as it is known then, also has to employ women although, as this image shows, polishing the fire engines' wing mirrors with a silk cloth and a powder puff is reckoned a suitable job for a woman.

Conscription helps to greatly increase the number of men in active service during the first year of the war but only just over 20 per cent of men are called up. This may not seem to be a large number but half the male population are children or too old for the initial recruitment. Take out those in the reserved occupations, government and civil servants required to run the country, those who are long-term sick or disabled, men of 'foreign' extraction of whom the authorities are wary and prefer not to enlist, and 20 per cent becomes quite an impressive number out of half the British population. So 10 per cent of the whole

Front cover of the *Home Companion* magazine, 6 January 1940

joins the armed forces, leaving 90 per cent of the population to fight on the Home Front.

In December 1941, Parliament passes a second National Service Act, widening the scope of conscription still further. It requires men up to 60 to do some form of National Service, which includes military service for those under 51 because there aren't enough men volunteering for police and civilian defence work, or women for the auxiliary units of the armed forces.

Conscription of women

This new act also makes all unmarried women and all childless widows (termed 'mobile' women) between the ages of 20 and 30 liable to be called up and given the choice of joining the services, the Women's Land Army or working in industry. Pregnant women, those with children aged under 14 or vital domestic responsibilities are not called up but, as 'immobile' women, they are encouraged to volunteer locally, perhaps working on the buses or railways or as delivery drivers.

The Auxiliary Territorial Service

Known as the ATS, this is the women's branch of the army and the most popular section to join is the Anti-Aircraft Command. The leaflet, *A Woman's Place – Now!* tells you all about it, the jobs you can train for, free time and 'leave' and, most important, how much the army will pay you. Unfortunately, though, the ATS has an image problem in that it's sometimes said all the girls seem to do is everybody else's dirty work and peel potatoes. In the early days, it's true that jobs are limited to cooks, clerks, orderlies, store-women and drivers but eventually there are a hundred or more different jobs open to women, from radio-location to the School of Army Experiments, from draughts-women to cinema projectionists. To begin with, the

A poster advertising the jobs women can now do. Australian National & Wikicommons

uniform isn't flattering either and one recruit reckons it makes her look like 'a sodden ginger pudding'.[1] In 1941, the army has a rethink on uniform, making it more shapely with a nipped-in waist and padded shoulders – much better – but the flat-heeled, brown, lace-up shoes remain because they're practical and comfortable, if unflattering, but then this is war; not a fashion show.

In the ATS, the starting pay is 1s 8d per day (for a man, it is 2s per day) but, as the recruiting leaflet is eager to point out, since all your living expenses – food, accommodation, medical and some travel expenses, uniform, etc. – are paid for you, this is your weekly pocket money, totalling 11s 8d, and it swiftly increases after a few weeks to 2s 10d per day, or even 3s 4d, depending on your job (for a man, it rises to 6s 3d). If you're promoted to a sergeant, you'll receive the daily rate of 4s 6d (6s for a man): that's £1 11s 6d per week to spend as you wish! This when, in 1942, half a pint of draught beer costs between 5d and 7½d, depending on which kind or brand you prefer. I'm afraid unequal rates of pay for doing the same job as a man are a fact of life for women at the time.

The First Aid Nursing Yeomanry

The First Aid Nursing Yeomanry or FANY – and trust me, nobody makes jokes about this acronym – has existed since the Great War and although it becomes amalgamated with the ATS, FANYs still reckon themselves to be rather different from the common ATS. Its members tend to be a bit posh, most of them can drive, their male family members are often top brass and many of the girls attended finishing school or travelled in Europe between the wars. They are invited to set up the Motor Driving Companies of the ATS, teaching others to drive. Because their male relatives are frequently brigadiers, rear admirals and other 'high-ups', FANYs, even of the lower ranks, are used to freely associating with officers and continue to do so, whereas this isn't allowed in the other services.

Those who spent time in Europe can often speak a number of languages quite fluently and these girls may make a very particular contribution to the war effort with their language skills. Translating enemy communications in German or Italian is vital or, far more dangerous, working as secret agents in occupied countries with the Special Operations Executive (SOE). Are your language skills good enough and do you have the courage to work for the SOE? If you answer yes to the first but prefer a safer option, there may be a place for you at Station X, better known since as Bletchley Park (see below).

The Women's Royal Naval Service

Known as the Wrens, this service existed during the Great War but was then disbanded only to be re-founded in September 1939. Every Wren is attached to a ship, even if her work is entirely land-based, and you'll have to refer to the floor as the 'deck' and your room is now your 'cabin'. On Thursday, 24 September 1942, Connie Miles notes in her

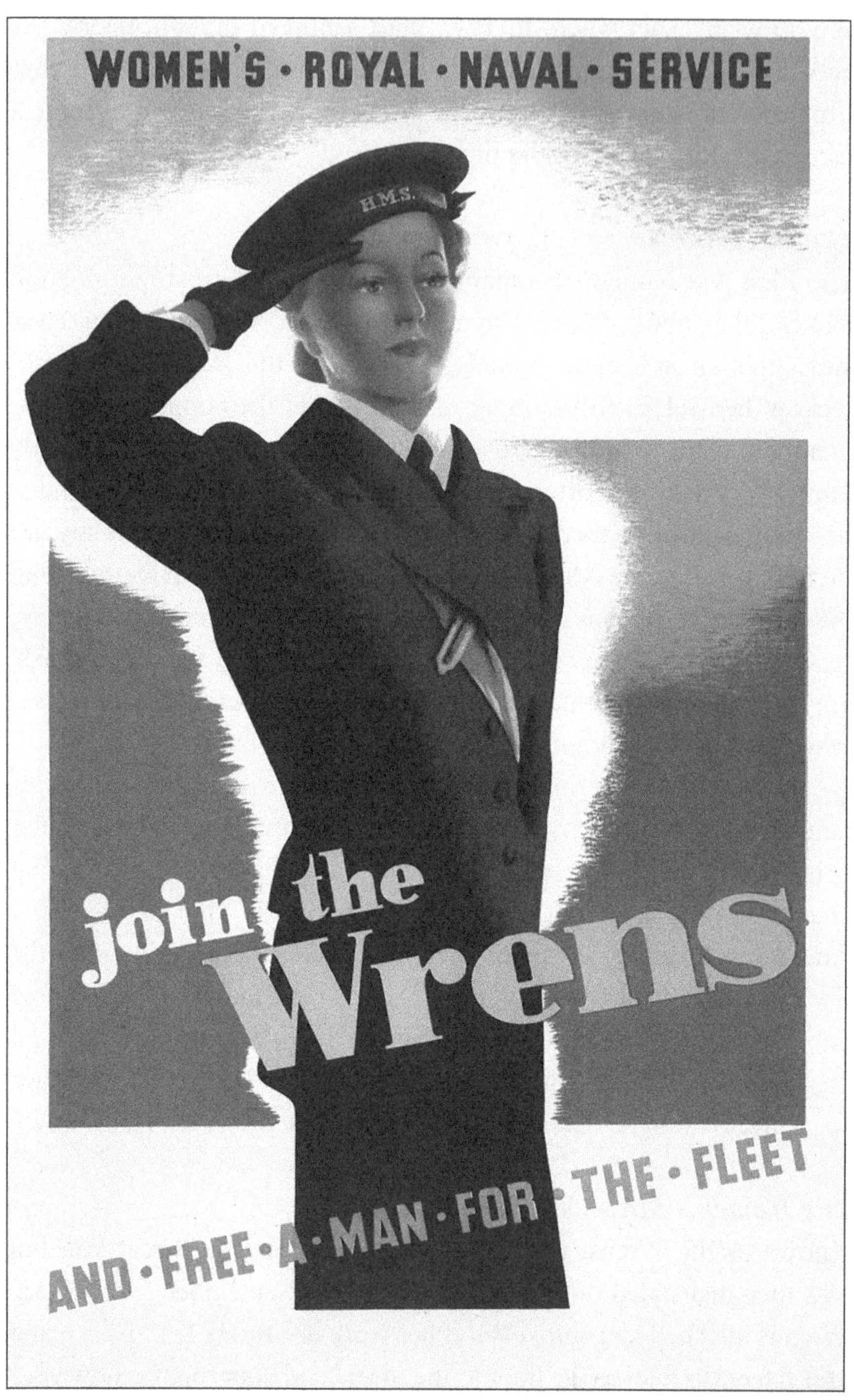

A 'join the WRENS' poster. Wikicommons

diary that her goddaughter has written to her. Petronelle, a newly joined Wren, writes: 'We are already steeped in naval terms and traditions. This building is HMS Pembroke III. I belong to Effingham division and sleep in No. 20 bunk, Cabin 3, Suffolk deck. It's fun.'[2] Incidentally, 'Effingham' was Lord Howard of Effingham, one of Queen Elizabeth I's admirals at the time of the Spanish Armada in 1588.

Your day is divided into three eight-hour 'watches'. Probationary Wrens do a fortnight's training course to learn drill, how to salute – the navy salute is made with the palm of the right hand facing the deck, not facing front as in the army – and the correct naval terms, as well as deciding which job will suit you best. Basic jobs include the usual women's tasks as cooks, clerical staff, wireless and telephone operators and parachute packers.

Most popular are the Signal and Transport Sections because details of every important naval or Fleet Air Arm (the navy's own air force) action come through the Signal Office. Wrens working here, dealing with coded messages or in the plotting room where ships' positions are constantly updated on huge maps, get the exciting – or traumatic – news first. The Transport Section includes dispatch riders, lorry drivers, motor mechanics and even chauffeurs for the top brass, so if you're a bit of a petrol-head this could be the place for you.

Compared to the ATS, the Wrens' uniform is far more stylish, in navy blue with a white shirt. The skirt is slightly flared rather than tapered like those of other services, to make it easier to step on or off boats and companionways. The design has King George's personal approval or, more likely, the queen's – she who, from 1952, is better known as the Queen Mother. She also approved the senior rating's and officer's tricorn hat after trying on various designs at Buckingham Palace. For some duties, Wrens are supplied with coveralls for dirty jobs, work dresses and aprons for cooks and laundresses, blue headscarves and berets and even trousers, if appropriate.

Also, unlike other services, the WRNS give you an allowance of £3 for underwear but the thick navy-blue woollen knickers – known as boiler-drawers – aren't popular. In 1940, an exceptionally cold winter, the thin raincoat is replaced with a heavy greatcoat. From 1941, Wrens serve on tugboats, harbour launches and other inshore vessels, so duffel coats, oilskins and sea boots are added to the kit as required and those thick knickers earn their place as thermal underwear.

As a Wren, you get twenty-one days' annual leave a year and a long weekend off every month, situation permitting. If you are reckoned 'exceptional' as a Wren and want extra excitement and more danger, you may get the chance to volunteer for service overseas.

The Women's Auxiliary Air Force

There had been a Women's Royal Air Force created along with the RAF in 1918 but the women's section disbanded just a year later. In 1939, it's realised that the RAF once again needs women to free up the men from desk jobs to fight and fly in combat, so the WAAF is formed. As usual, women can serve as cooks, waitresses, messengers, nurses, equipment assistants, drivers, telephone switchboard operators and office staff but in the summer of 1940, with the Battle of Britain raging in the English skies, job opportunities for women rapidly expand.

Now you have the chance to train in aircraft and radar plotting, manning and maintaining barrage balloons designed as airborne obstacles to confuse or entrap enemy planes, interpreting reconnaissance photographs, packing and repairing parachutes or debriefing returning RAF crews.

One concern of the male population is that 'women become too hysterical to be reliable in a crisis'. Nonsense, of course. Daphne Pearson proves that when, in May 1940, an RAF bomber, still fully laden, crash lands on Detling Airfield in Kent where Daphne is an Assistant Section Leader in the WAAF. She runs to open the gates for the fire crews and ambulances before rushing to the blazing plane. She climbs into the cockpit, revives the unconscious pilot, frees him from his parachute harness and drags him away from burning wreckage. As a 120 lb bomb explodes within the plane, Daphne shields the pilot with her body and then returns to try and save the rest of the crew but it's too late for them as more bombs explode. For her heroism, Daphne is promoted and awarded the new George Medal – the first woman to receive this military honour. Hysterical? I think not.

Although the Air Transport Auxiliary is actually a civilian organisation, they fly everything from Tiger Moths to Flying Fortresses. With too few male fighter pilots, women of the ATA actually get to fly Spitfires, Hurricanes, Lancaster bombers and such like, not in combat – that's definitely not allowed for women – but ferrying planes from the factory to the airfield or from one airfield to another, wherever they're most needed. The women often have very little flight training to begin with and new models are coming off the production line which they haven't flown before, so this is a case of seat-of-the-pants flying and learning on the job. However, the

Air Transport Auxiliary pilot, Diana Barnato Walker, climbs into a Spitfire. Wikicommons

planes fly without any armaments for defence against the enemy – which they may encounter – because the pilots are civilians. Is this something you could do? The pay is £8 per week, equal with the men, and the uniform is stylish with optional trousers! It sounds far more exciting than making tea in the canteen, doesn't it?

Let's ask an ATA pilot about her experiences.

'Excuse me, miss, could you tell us about your work for the ATA, please?'

'I suppose you think it's all glamour and excitement? Well, the only glamorous bit is my evenings spent in London, at various night clubs. Then I have to take a taxi back to the aerodrome in the small hours, grab an hour's sleep and be ready to collect my chit at 9.00 am sharp next morning.'

'Your chit?'

'Our instructions: whether we're flying a shot-up old Walrus that's barely air-worthy to the scrapyard for recycling or a brand-new Spitfire destined for Scapa Flow in the north of Scotland.'

'Can you fly anything?'

'If it's got wings attached, yes. We all know the basics and a flight engineer has put together a ring-binder explaining the differences in each kind of plane. Twenty minutes reading that and we're good to go. It was fortunate I'd read the notes for the Typhoon a month back because I was flying a well-used one across Wiltshire when the floor fell out of the cockpit and I could see the ground between my knees. I discovered that I couldn't fly it any slower than 230 mph or the engine would stall and then realised the undercarriage wouldn't lock. I was flying too fast to attempt a wheels-up landing but the notes I'd read earlier told me how to get the wheels down and, luckily, the green lights came on. I still had to land far too fast and without flaps, using a touch on the brakes to slow me down but it took the full length of the runway to stop.'

'I expect everyone congratulated you.'

'No. And I never even got a cup of tea because the plane was waiting to ferry me and the others back to base. That Typhoon never flew again.'

'What happens in bad weather?'

'We aren't supposed to fly if visibility is bad but sometimes it can't be helped. We aren't trained to fly using instruments only – although we have them, of course – but we have no radio so we can't be warned about bad weather up ahead. One evening at the club in London, my dear friend Max, a pilot, was appalled to learn that I hadn't been trained to fly on instruments which meant I'd be flying blind in fog. He took out his fountain pen, drew an instrument panel on the tablecloth and gave me a lesson there and then. It was so lucky he did because next day I was to fly a new Spitfire Mark IX. The weather was good when I took off but suddenly a blanket of fog came down. I made full use of what Max had taught me and managed to land safely. An RAF fellow congratulated me, saying I must be good on instruments. Little did he know.'

'It all sounds very dangerous.'

'I suppose it does but I love it. There's nothing to compare with flying on a clear day – the sense of freedom, the beauty of hills and lakes below you. Well, must dash: got to ferry a Halifax bomber to the scrapheap. Bye!'[3]

Another vital group of women, known as the Flying Nightingales, are nurses in the Air Ambulance Service and they do see action in the field as they are flown out to bring the wounded back from theatres of war to hospitals. Although the nurses are trained in the use of parachutes in case the aircraft is shot down, the parachutes are locked away for the return flight so the nurses have to stay with their patients come what may, with no chance of bailing out.

Did You Know?

The woman air ace, Amy Johnson, who flew solo from London to Australia in 1930, also flew planes with the ATA. During a flight, her plane disappeared off the RADAR over the Thames Estuary. She was never found.[4]

The Women's Land Army

The WLA isn't an army in the military sense and is run by the Ministry of Agriculture. However, it does have a uniform of sorts and sometimes the land girls work in secure areas under military law, such as on sites where camouflage experiments are underway. If this applies to you, you may have to sign the Official Secrets Act, just like a spy. This is the case at Kew Gardens where land girls grow camomile. This isn't to make a relaxing tea but to make turf lawns. Camomile is far more hard-wearing than grass and the idea is to cover airfields in camomile turf to disguise the runways. From above, to enemy pilots, they will appear to be nothing more than green fields.

The Land Army had existed during the Great War and is set up again in June 1939 when war seems inevitable. At first, joining is voluntary but, from December 1941, you can be conscripted into the WLA and by 1944 there over 80,000 'land girls'. If you love the outdoor life and don't mind working whatever the weather throws at you, this may be the job for you but you'll have to be prepared to work hard, doing anything from ploughing fields with a tractor or even horses, milking cows, cheese making, fruit-picking, mucking out the pigs, helping at lambing time, harvesting potatoes, rat-catching or anything else which needs doing on the farm. And the farm can be anywhere from Scotland to Cornwall.

Don't worry if you're a city girl and can't tell a lettuce from a dandelion; you'll receive training on the job and you won't be the only one as many girls from urban situations sign up for what is probably a 'healthy' option. On Friday, 24 July 1942, Connie Miles wrote in her diary:

> Petronelle, aged eighteen [who joins the WRNS in September, see above] is doing land work. She writes:
>
> 'We sleep on the ground on straw palliases. Isn't it surprising how quickly we become accustomed to things? Whereas ten days ago I would have screamed if I saw an earwig, I now nonchalantly pluck black beetles from my sponge, earwigs

from my pockets and spiders from my pillow. We go out to work for farmers in gangs. I have now risen to be forewoman of a gang. Girls are the gainers in this war.'[5]

A recruitment poster for the Women's Land Army. IWM

Land girls are paid by the farmers for whom they work and the pay isn't so good: 28s per week but half of that is taken back to cover your food and lodging. I'm afraid men get paid 38s! You'll work a forty-eight-hour week in winter and fifty hours in summer without any holidays but a free travel pass for a trip home after six months. Fortunately, in 1943, the 'Land Girls Charter' raises the minimum wage and introduces a week's holiday each year.

An unusual job for land girls is in East Anglia, where thousands of acres of fenland are being drained for crop growing. Here, you can be trained to drive bulldozers and excavators and other heavy plant machinery. Or what about joining the 6,000 girls of the Women's Timber Corps, felling trees and doing forestry work? This corps is set up in 1942 to supply urgently needed pit-props for mines, telegraph poles, and so on. Known as Lumber Jills, they're trained to select and measure suitable trees for felling – a bit of maths is required to work out the height of a tree using trigonometry – sawing the timber, transporting it from the forest to the road to be loaded onto lorries and clearing the forest floor of brushwood so saplings have a chance to thrive as well as reducing the risks of fires.

Factory work

If outdoor work doesn't appeal to you, maybe you'd prefer factory work? At least you won't be out in the rain but it's not an easy option and there's no equal pay for women.

Did You Know?

The Russians were our allies in World War II and a delegation from Russia came to visit England to see how our factories were producing tanks and armaments for use on the Russian Front. They were impressed by the products and the work ethic of the workers but were appalled that women were being paid less than men for doing the same job![6]

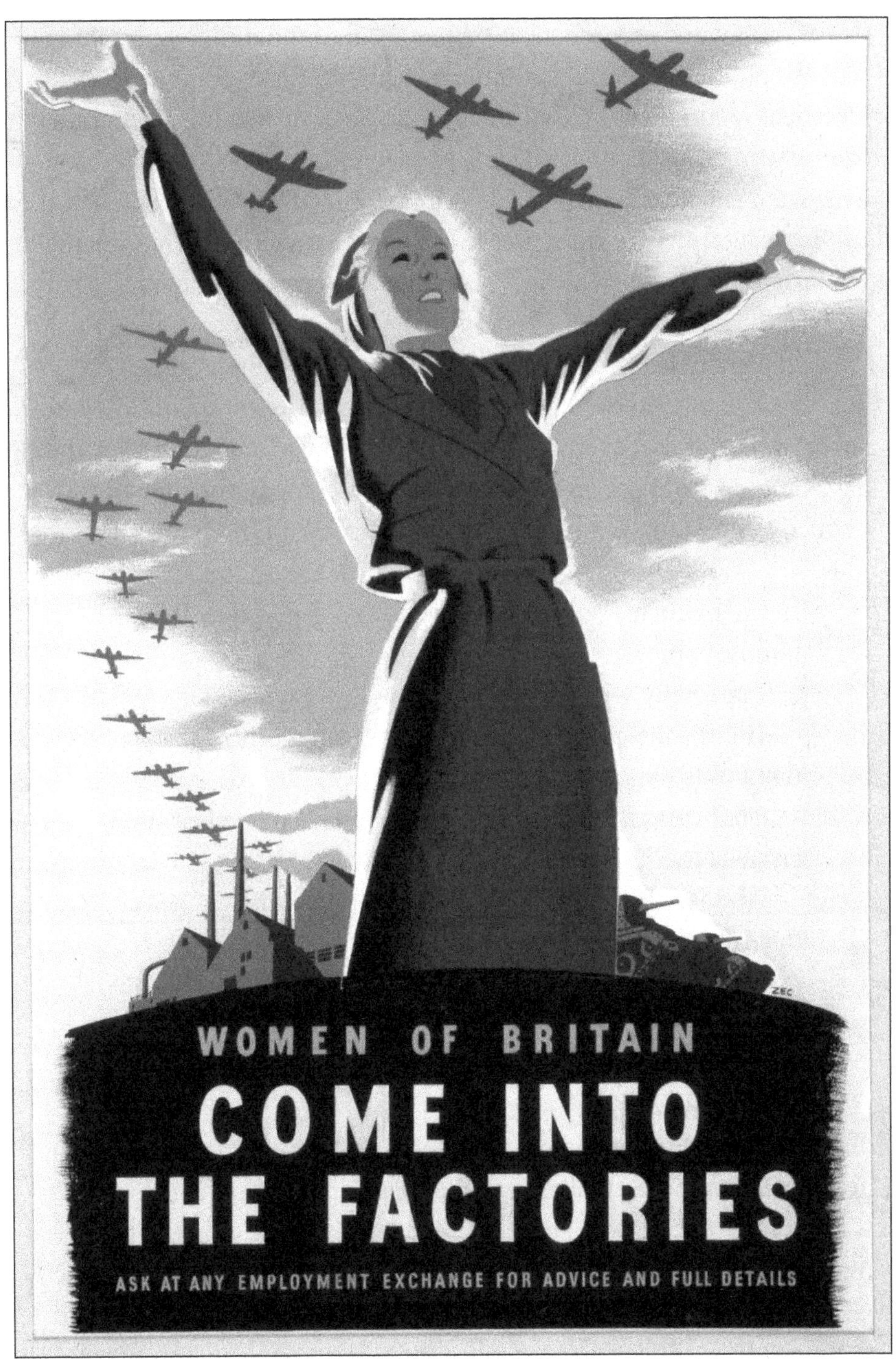

Recruitment poster for factory girls. TNA

Factory work can mean anything from shipbuilding to making bullets, producing cloth for uniforms or fire-hoses, manufacturing electrical components for radar or radio sets, or making medicines. Many women who have school-aged children who haven't been evacuated and aren't, therefore, eligible to be 'called up', still manage to fit in factory work during school hours, as well as caring for the youngsters, cooking, cleaning, shopping and doing the laundry. That takes dedication and a lot of energy.

You may be making nuts or bolts by the tens of thousands with no idea as to whether they're aeroplane parts or for use in scaffolding to shore up bomb-damaged buildings. Two popular entertainers of the day, Gracie Fields and Arthur Askey, sing a comedy song about this, entitled 'The Thing-ummy-bob'. Here are some of the lyrics:

> It's a ticklish sort of job making a thing for a thing-ummy-bob,
> Especially when you don't know what it's for.
> But it's the girl that makes the thing that drills the hole that holds the ring
> That makes the thing-ummy-bob that makes the engines roar.
> And it's the girl that makes the thing that holds the oil that oils the ring
> That makes the thing-ummy-bob that's going win the war.[7]

Bletchley Park

One area of work you cannot choose to do is the secret stuff which goes on at Station X, that is Bletchley Park in Buckinghamshire but, if your face fits or you have a particular skill, the powers that be may select you for this vital work. Everything which goes on at the Government's Code and Cypher School (GC&CS) is so hush-hush that nobody who works there talks about it and only in the twenty-first century do the full facts come to light. So if you do your research before you journey back to the 1940s, you'll know more than anyone, except perhaps the Prime Minister, Winston Churchill, about what goes on at Station X.

At Station X, enemy coded messages are deciphered, translated from German, Italian or Japanese into English and then assessed for their importance before being sent to whichever government department or military service needs to know. It's here at Bletchley that the first ever computers are invented to help with so much information to decode. You may be a whizz with a laptop but these computers are huge, filling entire rooms, clunky and, compared to a twenty-first century model, very slow. But they can analyse far more information faster than a human, if programmed and set up correctly. Using them is more about mechanics, electrics and typing skills and the answers come out of a teleprinter looking like noughts and crosses on paper, not on a monitor screen.

To decode top-level messages sent by Hitler to his high command across Europe, the Colossus is built. An enormous, noisy machine, only tall Wrens work on it because it stands so high. It works out 'Fish' encryptions from the German Lorenzo machines. You may have heard of the famous Enigma but Lorenzo is far more complicated and Colossus only does part of the job: hundreds of Wrens sit at school-type desks with pencils and paper doing the rest and they aren't told why or how their work with 'Fish' is useful to the war effort. In fact, it's vital. This is how one Wren describes Colossus:

> I met the Colossus just after I had signed the Official Secrets Act. I saw this astonishing machine the size of a room. It was ticking away and the tapes were going around and all the valves and I thought what an amazing machine. There were valves and transistors and flippy-flappy things. Like magic and science combined![8]

The computer is never switched off and must be attended around the clock. By the end of 1944, Station X has seven Colossus machines requiring constant attention and since the codes change every midnight, the night shift has to be alert and at the top of their game to begin working out the next day's Lorenzo code settings.

Conscription of men

Reserved occupations

So far, I've been suggesting the jobs women and girls can do to aid the war effort but not all men are conscripted into the armed forces. Certain occupations are 'reserved', that is they're vital to life on the Home Front. In April 1939, before war is declared, the Military Training Act is passed and men aged 20 and 21 are conscripted to complete six months' military training. At the outbreak of war, the National Service (Armed Forces) Act makes all men between 18 and 41 liable for conscription into the armed forces. However, in 1938 a Schedule of Reserved Occupations is drawn up, exempting certain key skilled workers from conscription. These reserved occupations include railway and dockworkers, miners, farmers, agricultural workers, schoolteachers, doctors and clergymen. Engineering jobs have the highest number of exemptions.

Some men in reserved occupations feel frustrated at not being allowed to go and fight, while those in the armed forces envy them for not being conscripted. Many in reserved occupations join civil defence units such as the Home Guard or the ARP, which creates more time-consuming extra responsibilities on top of their work. Often, their main occupations are by no means a soft option. Hours are long, conditions often difficult and some workplaces, such as factories and dockyards, are prime targets for enemy bombing. Also, if you're in a reserved occupation, you can be transferred to another site in the UK if your skills are needed there. For example, some dockworkers are moved from Southampton to Clydeside in Scotland.

Coal-mining suffers the most severe shortage of manpower because although miners are exempt from call-up, young men are

A Bevin Boy. Paper Pic Image

not replacing those who have to retire due to ill-health, accident or old age. At this time, Britain requires coal to fuel its power stations to generate electricity, to produce coal-gas for industry, cooking and heating as well as to burn as a fuel in itself to warm houses, fire up steam engines and locomotives. Britain runs on coal!

The Bevin Boys

By 1943, the coal-mining industry is desperate for strong, young men and on 12 November, the Minister of Labour, Ernest Bevin, makes this radio broadcast aimed at sixth-form boys approaching the age of 18, to encourage them to volunteer to work in the mines when they registered for National Service on leaving school. He promises the students that, like those serving in the armed forces, they will be eligible for the government's further education scheme after their time down the pit:

> We need 720,000 men continuously employed in this industry. This is where you boys come in. Each one of you, I am sure, is full of enthusiasm to win this war. You are looking forward to the day when you can play your part with your friends and brothers who are in the Navy, the Army, the Air Force … But believe me, our fighting men will not be able to achieve their purpose unless we get an adequate supply of coal … So when you go to register and the question is put to you 'Will you go into the mines?', let your answer be, 'Yes, I will go anywhere to help win this war'.

But the sort of boys who stay on at school until they're 18 are those destined for university, not the kind who go down the pit when they leave school at 14 (15 after 1944). Perhaps it's not surprising then that this appeal for volunteers isn't successful so, in December 1943, Bevin decides to select men of call-up age by a ballot to work in the mines. These conscripted miners are known as 'Bevin Boys'.

They come from all backgrounds and work alongside experienced miners, doing the less skilled tasks such as unloading coal from the tubs. Some 21,800 young men become Bevin Boys, alongside 16,000 who choose coal-mining in preference to the forces, when they are called up. These latter are often those whose religion forbids taking up arms, such as Quakers. The first Bevin Boys begin working in the collieries, having completed three weeks' classroom training and two weeks on site, on 14 February 1944 and the last are still mining until 1948.

Unfortunately, because Bevin Boys don't wear uniforms, some become targets of abuse from the public who mistakenly think they're 'draft-dodgers' or cowards. They are often stopped by the police as having possibly deserted from the armed forces. After the war ends, unlike those who served in the military, Bevin Boys aren't awarded medals for their contribution to the war effort and official recognition by the British government doesn't come until 1995.

Now you have an idea of the jobs you can do – Chapter 8 has more ideas for voluntary work to help the war effort – what clothes would you wear? What is thought fashionable and which items are indispensable? How do you buy them? These are the matters we'll look at next.

Chapter 6

What Would I Wear?

The 1930s had been a time of gaiety and colour in the fashion industry. 'Dressing for dinner' in the evening was normal for all but the poorest households. Your wardrobe changed twice a year and magazines like *Vogue* kept you up to date. Shopping for clothes on the High Street was quite a recent idea and most women either made their own or had a dressmaker put them together and wearing the correct outfit for the occasion was as important, if not more so, than being fashionable. Yet these were years of mass unemployment with the worst-off wearing hand-me-downs until they fell into rags while the wealthy swanked about in Parisian *haute couture* and what you wore was the label as to *who* you were. But the war is about to change all that.

By 1941, about 25 per cent of the population becomes eligible to wear a uniform of some kind, as a member of the armed forces, the women's auxiliary services or the many uniformed voluntary organisations, including the Boy Scouts and Girl Guides movements. The textile industries and clothes manufacturers go into overdrive, producing so many uniforms that clothing for civilians is soon in short supply. Boots and shoes for the forces have the same effect on footwear for ordinary people.

But the forces also have to adapt to cloth being in short supply. The army, which used to have a uniform for every occasion, by 1940 limits its field uniform to battledress. The khaki jacket – called a blouse – no longer has cuffs, pleated pockets and a fly front to cover the buttons so as to reduce the material required and speed up production.

According to a Mass Observation Survey done in 1941, a middle-class woman has an average of seven dresses, two or three costumes (a matching skirt and jacket), three other skirts, three

Did You Know?

Mass Observation Surveys were conducted for the government by teams of paid volunteers during the war and into the 1950s. They observed, interviewed and chatted to ordinary people to discover what they felt about the situations of the day, how they behaved and whether they thought the government was handling things reasonably well. The results were used to improve methods of rationing, air-raid facilities, etc.

coats, a mackintosh and five or six pairs of shoes in their year-round wardrobe. A middle-class man has three suits, two overcoats and four pairs of shoes. A poor man may have one suit, one coat and one pair of shoes. Women of the poorest class might have a couple of homemade dresses or skirts, a coat and a pair of shoes or two.[1]

Clothes rationing

Clothes rationing comes as a surprise to many when it's introduced on 1 June 1941, but with raw materials in short supply and so many factories and their work forces needed for the war effort, perhaps they should have seen it coming. As with food rationing, the government hopes to make things fairer for poorer families. Better-off people who take in evacuees from slum areas of London and Liverpool are shocked when some of the children arrive permanently 'sewn into' their only set of clothes!

The rationing scheme works by giving clothing 'points' values depending how much material of what kind and the labour involved in its production. A dress requires eleven points or coupons, a man's shirt or trousers eight – plus the monetary cost of the garment, of course. Men's shoes take seven and women's five, with stockings requiring two coupons. At first, every adult has sixty-six points for the year, but this is reduced as the war drags on.

Top Tip

If you don't want to use up coupons on stockings or they're unavailable, Mum told me they used to dust their legs with cocoa powder and because all stockings then had a seam up the back you got a friend with a steady hand to draw a seam line with an eyebrow pencil from knee to ankle or as much of your leg as showed. All was fine so long as it didn't rain and cover your legs in smears of chocolate, but at least they never laddered.

The cosmetics firm Cyclax of London invent a tinted cream called 'Stockingless cream' which may survive the rain rather better, if you find some available for purchase.

Babies' and childrenswear

There are no extra coupons for wedding dresses or maternity wear so clothes for these big events are carefully chosen with the idea of wearing them afterwards. Du Barry offer a coupon-free remodelling service on their maternity wear but every new mother receives fifty coupons for the baby's 'layette' – an old-fashioned word for the clothes needed by a baby, including shawls and dozens of nappies.

There are no disposable nappies and the muslin and terry towelling ones have to be washed after every soiling, dried and reused. That's an awful lot of laundry and there are no tumble dryers to overcome the problem of the British weather. As Eileen Gurney, a mother of two small children, wrote to her husband John, who was serving in the forces:

> I have hundreds of wet nappies on the line so I am just praying the rain will hold off till they dry. I wage an eternal war against the weather, trying to get the washing dry each day. At the moment the weather is definitely winning.[2]

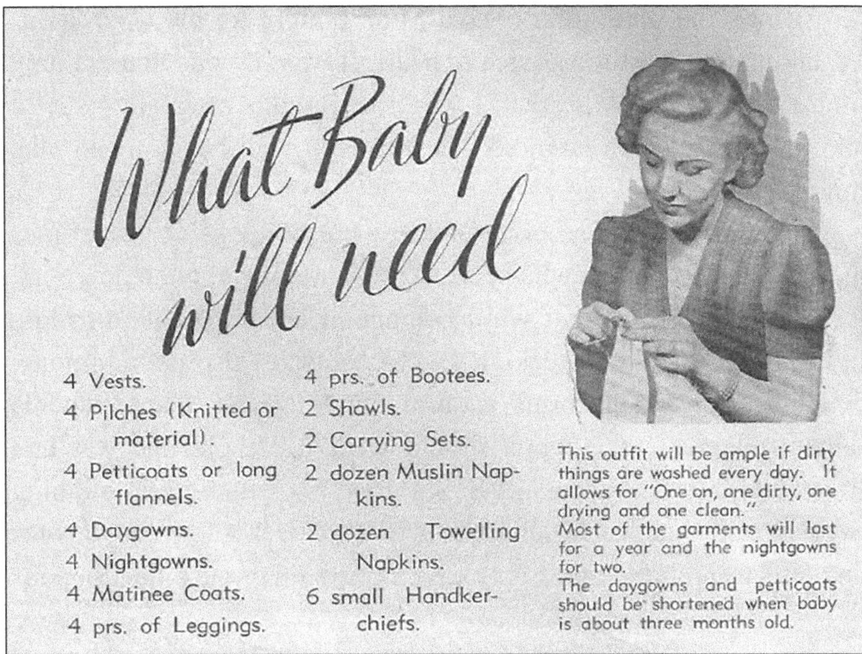

A baby's layette. Viyella

A pilch is like a pair of pants which helps to keep the nappy in place and, depending on the material used, hopefully reduces leaks, but a knitted pilch won't do much to keep in the wetness. And for all that knitting, even a 2 oz ball of wool requires one coupon. As far as I can discover, a carrying set consists of a long coat, often lacy in design, with matching bonnet and mittens and possibly other accessories. Such a set is for special occasions like baby's first visit to grandparents, the christening and other events where the parents want to carry around and show off the newest arrival. However, there is no mention on this list of that vital item: the bib, and how much washing that might save!

For older children, fortunately their clothes require fewer coupons than those for adults as the government realises that youngsters always grow and need new ones. Even so, parents are advised to buy clothes of a larger size than immediately needed for the children to 'grow into'. On a personal note and true, I never did 'grow into' the school duffel coat Mum bought for me when I was 11, taking that wartime advice to heart. It was so wide that the only time I filled it out was when I was nine months pregnant aged 24 and again two years later, so it lasted very well but you can take things a bit too far.

In 1942, children receive an extra ten coupons or sometimes more for the teenagers who seem to grow weekly, though don't call them 'teenagers', as that word belongs at least a decade or more in the future. Children reckoned to be 'outsize' also get additional coupons. School uniforms require coupons and many schools remain adamant that pupils should wear it, despite the war and limited supplies. But the WVS is a great help, setting up clothing exchange schemes in which parents receive back a few coupons for any still wearable clothes they give in and then reuse the coupons to buy larger sizes.

Fashion goes on the ration

Regarding clothing coupons, the government makes special provisions for manual workers whose clothes will become worn out, for civilians in the voluntary services who have to buy their own uniforms, for diplomats who must dress to impress foreign envoys and, surprisingly, for theatre performers who require costumes. You'll find advice about the complicated coupon system on posters, in official leaflets and in magazines. The change from free-spirited fashion to practical, functional clothing is swift. With everyone expected to carry their gas mask with them everywhere, high-quality leather shoulder bags with a compartment for the stylish woman to keep her mask become the must-have accessories. But not changing your daytime outfit to something more up-market for the evening is still frowned upon. You're 'letting yourself go and letting other people down', if you go to nightclubs or restaurants in 'hairy sweaters and flannel bags', or even if you stay at home for the evening.

These 'flannel bags' or 'slacks', as they are known, are new to British fashion. Previously, women have always worn skirts and if they did wear trousers for cycling or a similar activity, they might be refused service in cafés or bars. But in the 1940s, film stars like Lauren Bacall, Katharine Hepburn and Marlene Dietrich are photographed looking glamorous wearing trousers. It's a revolution and with so many women now employed in the factories, doing farm work or digging allotments, wearing trousers has become not only a practical daytime option but, if made of silk or velvet, an acceptable choice for evening wear too.

Another new variation on trousers is the 'siren suit', so called because it's a 'onesie' you can pull on quickly over your night clothes while you're still half asleep, if the air-raid siren has you rushing for the shelter in the small hours. They're available for men as well and the Prime Minister Winston Churchill makes the siren suit his trademark, along with the cigar, but being rather rotund, he isn't the best shape to make it a real fashion statement.

Vogue patterns for trousers and siren suits to make your own. Vogue Pattern Book

Which items are indispensable?

In October 1940, with your dress allowance already somewhat reduced from the sixty coupons you received in June, *Housewife* magazine advises the stylish woman on her winter wartime wardrobe and check or tweed is a 'must':

- First and most important, your top coat. Its line and colour will influence every other item so choose carefully. Fur-trimmed and 'dressy' styles are out. First class fabric is in. Nothing extreme as you're buying for more than one season and it'll go out of fashion.
- If your coat is plain, buy a check suit, i.e. a skirt and jacket. Add a tailored wool crepe shirt in the suit's dominant colour and a crepe-de-Chine shirt/blouse in another of the tones. Knit yourself a couple of gay woollies to go with the suit.
- Two day-dresses. A shirt-frock for work-a-day wear, perhaps checked, if your coat is plain, should have a high neckline with turn-down collar and nothing more fussy than pin-tucks or pockets. A fine woollen frock suitable for a social lunch or tea or a quiet evening with friends should be in a plain colour and can have some fullness in the skirt. Both should have hemlines 17 or 18 inches from the floor and have narrower silhouettes than last season. This is the new fashion and only partly due to wartime shortages.
- Note. This list doesn't include an evening dress but, if you must have one, choose a simple style and sew it yourself.

An interviewee for the Women's Land Army informed the formidable director, Lady Denham, who was to meet the young woman when she arrived by train from London, that she would be able to recognise her because she would be wearing pink. Lady Denham felt anxious about anyone who thought pink was a suitable shade for the countryside, it being definitely a 'city colour'. But all was well; no fashion *faux pas* was committed here because she was dressed in smart pink tweed and tweed can be worn anywhere.[3]

British fashion: lots of tweeds and checks. Getty Press Photo

Accessories

Most surprisingly, the wardrobe mentioned above doesn't include hats but, trust me, they are essential to the well-dressed woman, as you can see in this photograph. Hats aren't rationed but become absurdly expensive so to save money you can always make your own. Women's magazines often have ideas and give instructions for creating all kinds of headwear, from gluing felt and braid to make and trim a fashionable pill-box hat to crocheting or knitting a 'saucy' snood in silky bouclé yarn. For work, wearing a headscarf turban-style is popular and safety-conscious, keeping long hair from becoming entangled in machinery.

Gloves add a finishing touch to any outfit and you'll need a handbag (purse), of course. Handbags tend to be quite large during the 1940s because you need somewhere to keep your ID card, ration book and coupons and any other paperwork often required, plus the usual 'stuff' we women acquire and possibly your gas mask as well, although these are carried less and less frequently as the fear of gas attacks dwindles.

The posh London store of Fortnum and Mason advertises: 'We now stock dungarees in which you can tackle a man's job, split cycling skirts and white mackintoshes which, quite apart from their valuable waterproof qualities, lessen the risk of blackout collisions.' Although the scarcity of cloth limits designs, luckily colour isn't rationed and bright patterns are highly prized, cheering up the sad greyness of war-battered Britain.

Underwear

Silk underwear is best if you can get hold of this gorgeous textile. You'll probably hear about parachute silk, i.e. from parachutes too damaged for further use, being made into luxurious nightwear, bras, French knickers and even wedding dresses. A set of underwear is made by a dressmaker for a customer using a silk map given to the customer by her boyfriend in the RAF. Flight crews are given these maps, which are light and easily hidden in a sock in case they are shot down and have to find the way home.

Camiknickers are very fashionable but not so practical as they're a 'onesie' version of a camisole and knickers. (Do you have to completely undress every time you need the loo? Just asking.) Women also make nightdresses, tea towels and baby clothes from cheesecloth, butter muslin and curtain net which are not rationed.

You may be surprised to learn that most women, like their Edwardian mothers and Victorian grandmothers, wear corsets, even those who are slim. Corsets come with suspenders attached to hold up your stockings. Because they are rubberised and rubber is needed for tyres for the war effort, new corsets are in short supply. Fear not, the Board of Trade produces a leaflet on '8 ways to make Corsets wear longer'. Hints include: *Always wear a thin vest beneath your corsets as perspiration soon weakens and rots elastic and rubber fabric and the vest will absorb it. At night, spread your corsets over a chair-back to air them. Wash them once a fortnight but never scrub or rub, just squeeze in warm suds*. But, if your corsets need more help, *Good Housekeeping* magazine, in 1943, recommends an old corset renovating service, price 12s 6d.

Menswear

Men's clothes don't excite the fashion-conscious although, pre-war, David, Prince of Wales, who was, briefly, King Edward VIII in 1936, was a trend-setter in his plus-fours, Oxford bags, checked jumpers and Windsor-knotted ties. The man-about-town usually wears a bowler hat and, even when dressed casually, never goes without a collar and tie.

Two or three suits are a must, usually three-piece which means a jacket, trousers (pants) and waistcoat (vest). You'll want a town suit in wool, a country suit in tweed and a Sunday best suit for going to church, weddings, christenings and funerals. As you buy a new Sunday best every few years, your previous suit can be demoted to your town suit. For informal occasions, you can leave off the waistcoat and wear a knitted jumper, pullover or cardigan under your suit jacket and replace the formal bowler with a trilby or, in the country, a flat cap or deerstalker. Flannel bag trousers are worn for sport and holidays. All trousers have a button fly – no zip fasteners – and are held up with braces (suspenders). Blazers are for summer wear and sporting events, even if you're merely a spectator, when it may be permitted to have your top shirt button undone and abandon your tie, but such occasions are rare.

For evenings, dinner jackets were vital before the war but as so many men are in uniform by 1940, this custom becomes less common. And abandoning your dinner jacket is only one item of change but now there are more drastic changes coming.

Utility clothing

Each type of clothing requires the same number of coupons whatever the quality. Only the monetary cost changes, so a silk dress will cost more than a cotton one but both need eleven coupons. Whereas food rationing makes things fairer for the less well-off, clothes rationing doesn't. In fact, it's worse for those who can only afford cheaper garments because they're of poorer quality, wear out sooner and so require coupons to buy replacements more often and everyone has the same number of coupons, regardless of income. Utility clothing of decent quality and well made, sold at fixed prices, is intended to solve this unfairness.

In May 1942, the first Civilian Clothing Restriction Order changes fashions drastically. Men's suits pre-war had made use of plenty of cloth but now jackets can only be single breasted, not double, no buttons or slits at the cuffs and no flaps on the pockets. Trousers cannot have turn-ups nor more than three pockets, no elastic in the waistband – elastic uses rubber which is needed for tyres and tank

This CC41 or 'double cheese' mark becomes a common feature not only on furniture from 1941, as per the logo (see Chapter 2) but from 1942 it appears on the new range of Utility clothing. Public Domain

> ## Did You Know?
>
> The buttons on the cuff served no purpose but were the retailer's quick guide to the price and quality of the suit: three or four buttons denoted top notch; two buttons mid-range and one button cheapest. My dad, being among the very first to join up in 1939, was one of the first to be 'de-mobbed' from the Royal Navy as a Chief Petty Officer in 1945. The demob suit which he was given must have been made pre-war since it had trouser turn-ups and pocket flaps and wide lapels on the double-breasted jacket. Made of top-quality mid-charcoal grey wool with a chalk stripe, he was still wearing it for best in the 1960s.

tracks – and no zips, so only button flies allowed. The trouser legs are straighter; less flared than before.

The number of buttons is limited on women's clothes as well, as is the number of pleats and no pocket flaps, button-down pockets, frills nor turn-back cuffs. Excessive top-stitching and embroidery are banned, as are certain materials. Hems must just cover the knee and no longer than that. In 1943, elastic is limited to being used in corsets and knickers only and then as little as possible. Rather than all around the waist, a short length is used on either side in knickers.

Because of the shortage of rubber, rubber soles are banned on shoes, as is the rubberised adhesive used in their manufacture and metal buckles. So as not to waste leather, cut-out designs and peep-toes are no longer made. Soles and heels are now of wood, the former requiring a new way of walking, putting your toe to the ground first, not your heel, because the sole doesn't flex and bend. The latter must be no more than a fraction over two inches high and cannot be covered in leather. If you're in need of rubber gloves or Wellington boots for the work you do, you'll need a purchase permit from your employer to get them and, even so, they're in short supply.

But it's not all bad news for the fashion-conscious. Utility clothing is stylish and comfortable, well made and meant to last.

Our twenty-first-century throwaway attitude to clothes would be inexplicable, unpatriotic and illegal in the 1940s.

Skirts are shorter and straighter, collars smaller and buttons fewer – or none at all, as in the jacket second from the right. Shoulders are squarer, more like those of uniform jackets, but it's a smart look. Any off-the-peg clothing has rocketed in price since war began but if you have a bit of know-how, patterns are available to make your own. Although this is a much cheaper option, you'll still need coupons to buy the material but, early on, upholstery cloth isn't on the coupon and some of it is suitable to make hard-wearing clothing, so get there quickly, before it's sold out.

If you haven't a clue about dressmaking, fear not, the Women's Institute (WI), the WVS and even the Girl Guides offer lessons on the subject, as well as knitting and crochet classes, so you can learn how to use a pattern, adapt it to your size and customise your new

Utility wear. University of Lincoln

outfit with bits gleaned from elsewhere, such as contrasting inserts or collars or patch pockets.

Marion Cashman remembers her mum going to jumble sales to buy old knitted items to unravel and to collect the buttons for reuse, keeping them in the 'button tin'.[4] I recall my nan had a button tin too which we inherited – sorting buttons was a good game when I was little. My nan also went to jumble sales to buy second-hand clothes to unpick and remake or use as patches or inserts to make new garments. Bits of lace trim or ribbons were avidly collected off old items to adorn plain Utility wear. But be aware: even buying second-hand clothing requires a few coupons. However, use your imagination freely to create your own look. Recycle and be innovative in making your own accessories to suit your outfit.

The 'Make Do and Mend' campaign encourages everyone to make the most of the clothes they already have in the back of the wardrobe and to care for them so they last well and in good condition.

Utility patterns are available to make your own. McCall's (pattern 1) and note the contrasting inserts in the left-hand image of pattern 2 by Du Barry

Top Tip

As you won't have a pre-war wardrobe to update, you may want to visit a vintage clothing shop or a charity shop (thrift shop) before you journey back and take some suitable styles with you. You have the advantage of knowing when clothing rationing is going to happen, so you can get ahead of the game, fashion-wise.

Posters, leaflets and magazine articles offer advice on keeping and storing clothing and moth balls are a must since most garments are of natural fibres, although nylon and rayon have been invented. Nylon stockings are a GI's best gift for a girlfriend and the quick-drying, easy-care, moth-proof qualities of the new rayon are advertised in fashion magazines, but both are almost impossible to buy during the war. Knowing how to renovate and repair what you already have becomes an ever more vital skill.

It's wasteful and unpatriotic to throw away clothes and 'Make Do and Mend' becomes the catchphrase of the later years of the war. Patching, knitting, darning and adjusting are the order of the day. Even among the wealthy, it becomes patriotic to dress in clothes which look revamped from a pre-war garment. Some women wear men's clothes while their men are away and in uniform. One woman greets her husband wearing 'his pants (a bit of lace had made them into knickers), his shirt, his pyjama jacket as a blazer and a skirt made from a bleached food stuff bag, and a belt made from Cellophane. And he never even noticed.'[5]

Beauty is your duty

It is now unfashionable to be wearing 'showy' clothes but the fashion magazines insist that women 'do not let standards slip too far'. The government is concerned that a scruffy appearance could be a sign of low self-esteem and morale and might have a serious impact on the war effort. Women's morale becomes a major factor in government thinking. A bold face is essential to survive life on the Home Front and for this reason cosmetics are not rationed, although they're in short supply, expensive and subject to a tax on luxury goods.

Their houses and families may be ravaged by the scourge of war, but the women of Britain are determined that their appearances shouldn't suffer the same fate. Whether at home or involved in war work, every effort is made to keep their looks, whatever the conditions. The British cosmetics company Yardley actually has little make-up available for sale but does its bit for the war effort with advertisements like the one shown.

In a Yardley cosmetics advertisement from October 1942, the text says:

> We cannot have it both ways. Even if we were not called to help, we could not leave men to fight this war alone. We asked for equal rights and we cannot have it both ways. It is only fair that we should face the music side by side with our men. Total war makes heavy demand on us. We must submit to routine and still keep the sparkle of unfettered days. We must take risks and show no sign of fear. We must work hard and let no weariness appear. We must remember that the slightest hint of a drooping spirit yields a point to the enemy. Never must careless grooming reflect a mood of laissez faire. Now that leisure and beauty-aids are limited, we can take pride in looking our best. Face value is more than ever high. Never should we forget that good looks and good morale are the closest of good companions. Put your best face forward.[6]

Manufacturers of beauty products switch production to things needed for the war effort. Coty of London, for example, who used to produce

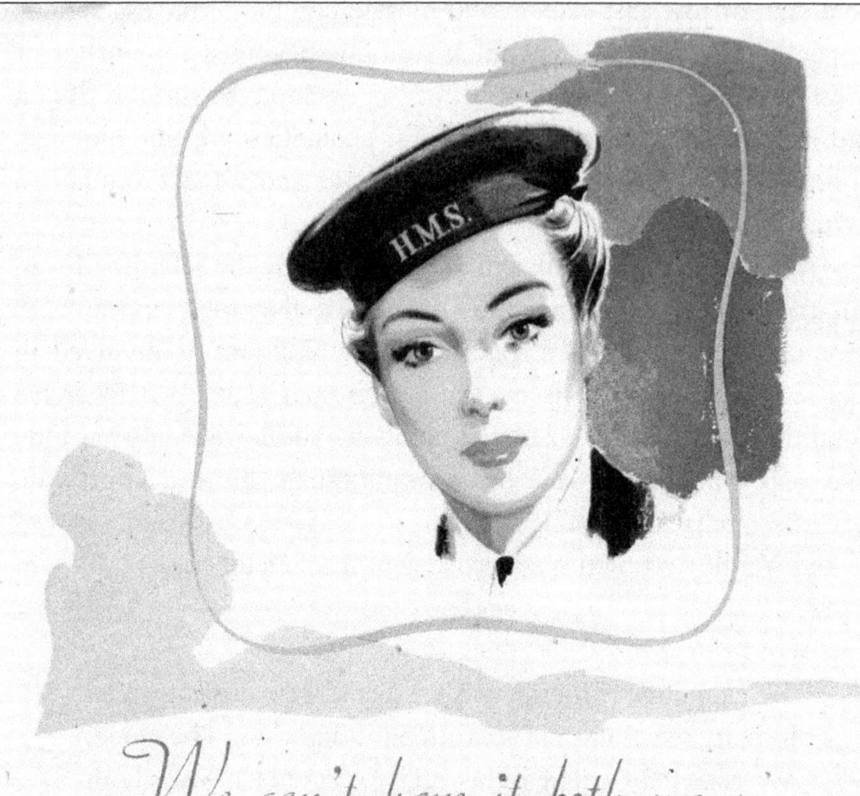

A Yardley advertisement, October 1942

perfumes and face powder, now make foot powder for the army and anti-gas blister ointment. Some companies go as far as to admit that make-up is in short supply but assure customers there will be plenty available after the war. No wonder advertisements in magazines like *Good Housekeeping* advise readers to 'Cherish your Perfume and Treasure your Powder'.

My mum, Joyce, has a few tips which are pretty clever ways to 'make do' and improvise with make-up. Let's ask her about them:

Interview with Joyce Botting, née Thomas

'Hello, Mum, what can you tell us about ways of looking good when make-up is so hard to get?'

'Well, there's no good substitute for that necessity: face powder. But if you run out completely, talcum powder can take the unfashionable shine off your nose, although it's white and makes you too pale. So a dab of beetroot juice on your cheeks makes a good rouge, or blusher, as you call it now.'

'What about eye make-up? My eyelashes are so fair, what can I do about them?'

'You know eyebrows are more important to fashion in the forties than lashes but I've heard that shoe polish can be applied with a mascara brush to darken lashes and eyebrows. I haven't tried it myself. I think it might smear rather horribly, though.'

'What about lipstick? Everyone wears that in the 1940s, don't they?'

'Yes, dear. You can't go out without lipstick, you know. It would be like appearing in public half undressed; letting the side down. I'll tell you about my friend Peggy. She puts on her lipstick *before* she goes to bed…'

'Why on earth…'

'Obviously, because if the air-raid siren goes and she has to rush out to the shelter… And she keeps it in her dressing gown pocket so nobody will see her without her lipstick in the middle of the night, even in an emergency. Never mind that her dressing gown is of patched and faded candlewick from an old bedspread and her slippers are lined with newspaper.'

'Do you wear lipstick at night, Mum?'

'Well, er, no. It's too precious to waste and besides, who can see it in the blackout? But here's a great tip for you: I save my lipstick stubs when they're too worn down to use, melt them all together in a saucepan and pour the mixture back into a lipstick tube to cool and set. The result is a new and unique shade of lipstick that nobody else can copy. Good idea, eh?'

'Thanks, Mum, I'll remember that. Bye!'

Unfortunately, one truly basic 'cosmetic' does go on the ration: toilet soap. As noted in *Instructions for American Servicemen in Britain, 1942*, soap and shampoo are now so scarce that factory girls cannot get the grease off their hands or out of their hair. The Palmolive advertisement shown has a Hollywood air about it, making their toilet soap sound glamorous and exotic. And perhaps it has become so rare as to be an 'exotic' commodity. Even so, using it can be your contribution to the war effort, keeping up a serving man's morale. Professional portrait photographs are often something which girlfriends, sweethearts and wives send to their loved ones in the forces.

At least doing your hair differently is a cheap option for changing your look. Wearing it either short or up is as much a safety measure as a fashion statement, if you're doing factory or farm work. Accidents caused by long hair getting caught in machinery are something to guard against.

So now you know what to wear and the complications of getting hold of the clothes you want. You're aware of how looking good can raise your morale and that of others, but what else can you do to keep calm and carry on? This is the topic for the next chapter.

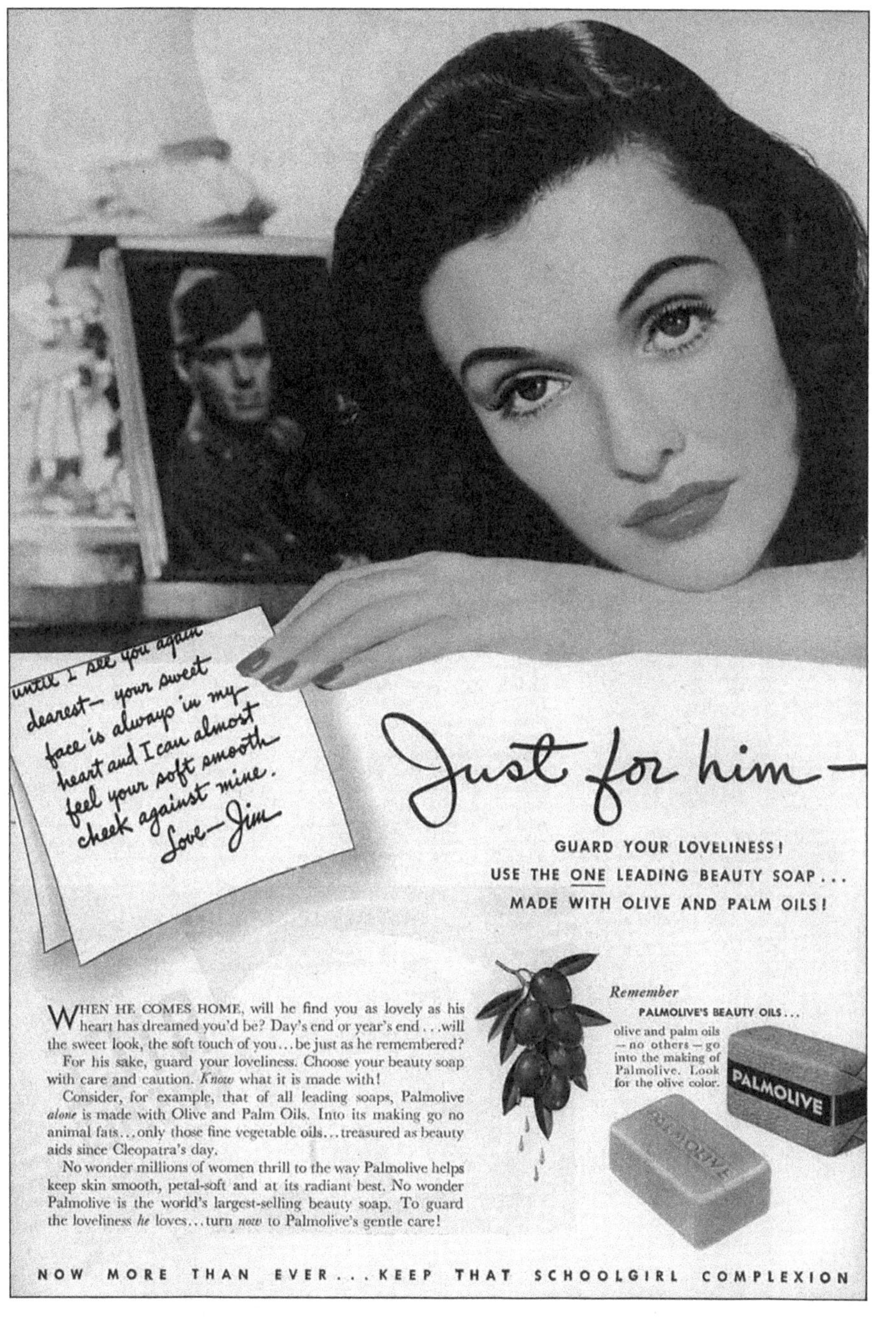

A Palmolive toilet soap advertisement says to keep beautiful for him while he's away

Chapter 7

How Could I Keep Calm and Carry On?

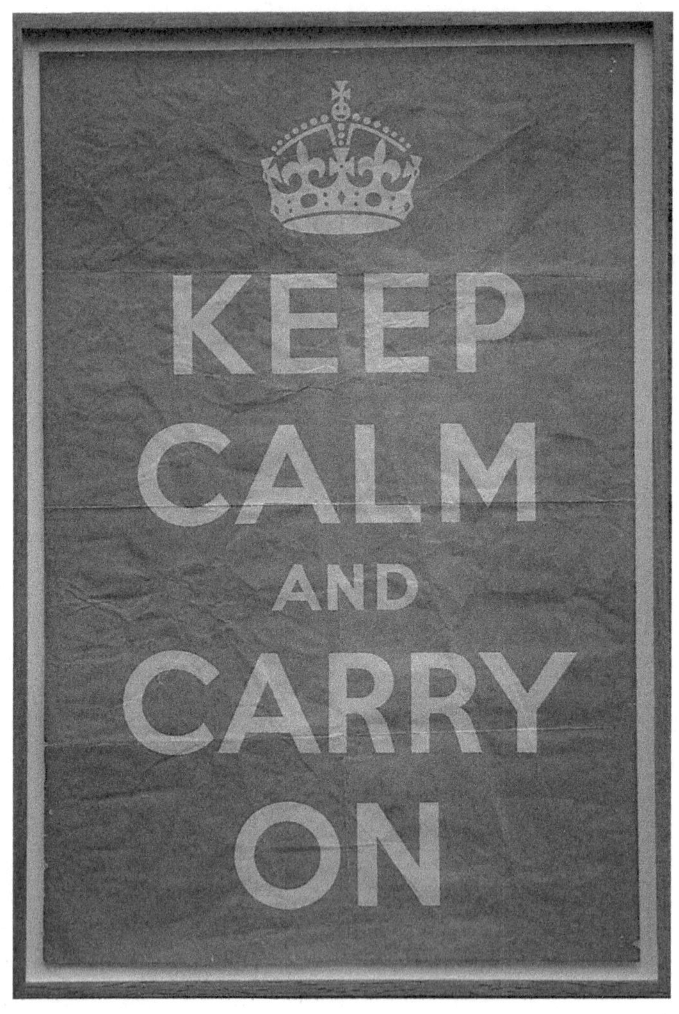

'Keep Calm and Carry On' poster. This famous poster was produced but never actually used during the war. Wikicommons

The fashion magazine *Vogue* says that it's a woman's duty to practise the 'arts of peace' in wartime so such activities don't die out and become lost when peace returns. To do this, it continues, the magazine's pages are dedicated to encouraging an intelligent and useful attitude to everyday affairs and to bringing as much cheer and charm into our lives as possible.

This chapter looks at the incredible efforts that are made to live in a way that's as 'normal' as possible amongst the upheavals and dislocations of war. What can you do to help keep up morale, enjoy what little leisure time you have, carry on at the Home Front and work towards peaceful times in the future?

Recreation

That generous man, Lord Nuffield, who supplies servicewomen with free sanitary products, also provides sports equipment for games including darts, table tennis and badminton. In addition, he gives libraries and wireless sets to entertain and keep the forces cheerful, including the Territorial Army and Auxiliary Services at home. Impressed by the number of volunteers recruited from as early as May 1939, before compulsory conscription begins, he sets up clubs for service personnel, offering meals, accommodation, variety shows featuring the best artists of the day, dances and complimentary theatre tickets.

He founds the Nuffield Trust to keep up his good work with rest and recuperation schemes for exhausted air crew and for women serving in particularly difficult and hazardous situations, such as members of the SOE who work undercover in occupied Europe. Many of the Trust's innovations continue in the twenty-first century.[1]

Of course, Lord Nuffield, as the founder and owner of the Morris Motor Manufacturing Company, is a very wealthy man and much of the funding for his charitable efforts is in the form of donated shares in his extremely profitable company which makes engines for tanks, among other things. But how can you, with just a few shillings to spare, help keep up morale?

Dancing

Can you dance? I don't mean hip-hop or whatever is the latest 'set of grooves and moves' in the twenty-first century, although the GIs do introduce 'swing' dancing and the jitterbug which are energetic and lively. This is mostly about ballroom dancing. If your answer is 'no', I suggest you take a few lessons in the waltz, quickstep and foxtrot before you journey back in time. It'll be worth the cost and effort, I promise, because just about everybody can dance in the 1940s and it's a great way to socialise and make friends. There are usually live bands, from full orchestra in large dance halls to three-piece bands in smaller ones although, in the village hall, you may have to make do with the church organist who can also play the piano or, in desperation, somebody's wind-up gramophone (record player).

In 1939, when war is first declared, dancehalls, cinemas – often called 'picture houses' or simply 'the pictures' – theatres and other places of public entertainment are closed for safety reasons. You can see the point: hundreds of people trying to get out if the air-raid siren sounds or in the events of a gas attack could cause as many casualties as the enemy's bombs. However, the Brits, being a determined bunch, make widespread protests against the closures, insisting that the nation needs entertainment to keep up its spirits. Realising this is

> **Top Tip**
>
> A group of members of a Young Farmers Club have a way of getting around the ban on going by car. When they wish to hold a dance, they have a quiz or a lecture beforehand because you are still permitted to drive cars to an 'educational' event. Then, when the quiz or talk is ended, they stay on and have the dance afterwards. This is a tip you might like to pass on.

true, the government changes its mind and, within a fortnight out of town and a month in London, most places have reopened.

One difference is that, apart from so many partners, male and female, now wearing uniform, it's illegal, because of petrol rationing, to use a private vehicle to get to an event as frivolous as a dance, even if the rain is pouring down, soaking your nice dress or smartest uniform and ruining your hairdo.

Football

The English Football League season began, as usual, in August 1939 but is suspended on 3 September with the outbreak of war. But just as with those who enjoy dance and theatre, football fans object strongly to being denied the chance to watch their favourite teams in action and the season starts up again at the end of October but not in the usual way. Because the government has limited travel to no more than fifty miles, all games have to be local, so regional league competitions

World War II football fans at Wembley for England v. Scotland match. Football Association

are set up instead. The Northern League actually completes an entire season of match fixtures.

But another problem for the sport is that the players are all fit young men and more and more of them are called up to serve in the forces. The depleted teams are made up with 'guest' players. For example, the London club, Crystal Palace, fields 186 different players on its side during the war years. Despite air raids, the crowds at these matches are huge, including young boys – I'm afraid football at this time is 'men-only' for both players and spectators – and play continues uninterrupted, though many keep their gasmasks and tin helmets handy, just in case.

Fortunately, normal play is resumed for the 1945–1946 season but, sadly, with many of the previous star players now missing. But amateur games continue throughout and the armed forces encourage their men to keep fit by playing football, cricket and tennis.

Cinema

The British film industry continues throughout the war, mostly making small budget black-and-white pictures either on a patriotic theme, such as *Ships with Wings*, or *In Which We Serve*: a film made in 1942 in colour, starring Noël Coward. Romance isn't forgotten, with films like *Brief Encounter* with Celia Johnson and Trevor Howard (1945), and comedies, such as *Bell-Bottom George*, starring George Formby (1944).

There are a few big budget British films such as *That Hamilton Woman* (1941), the story of Nelson and Lady Hamilton, starring Laurence Olivier and Vivien Leigh; Shakespeare's *Henry V* (1944), again starring Laurence Olivier in 1944 and *Caesar and Cleopatra* (1945) in which Vivien Leigh stars, though not to great acclaim. All these stories are given a strong patriotic element; as one viewer noted, *Caesar and Cleopatra* could well have been called *Churchill and Cleopatra* and ancient Rome renamed blitzed London.

In the US, Walt Disney is producing some of his most iconic feature-length animation films, including *Pinocchio* (1940), *Fantasia*

(1940), *Dumbo* (1941) and *Bambi* (1942). But the blockbuster movie of the war has to be *Gone with the Wind*, a Hollywood film starring the current heart throb, Clark Gable, as the rogue Rhett Butler and the English starlet, Vivien Leigh, as Scarlett O'Hara. Released in December 1939 in the US and here in Britain in February 1940, it runs throughout the war. Made in full Technicolor, it tells of a young woman left alone on the 'home front' in America's Deep South when all the menfolk have gone off to fight in the war. In this case, it's the American Civil War of the 1860s but viewers can empathise with the beautiful, beleaguered and doughty heroine, Scarlett.

When the cinemas first reopen after their brief closure in September 1939, anyone hoping to watch the films can be refused entry if they haven't got their gas mask with them, so don't forget yours, although the requirement is phased out quite quickly as the fear of a gas attack fades.

Every town has at least one cinema and probably three or four, each with a different programme, and most villages have access to films which may be shown in the village or church hall. In towns, tickets cost between 1 and 2 shillings, or cheaper in the countryside, but you'll certainly get value for money because you don't see just a single film. The black-and-white *Pathe Newsreel* with its crowing cockerel logo will keep you up to date with the progress of the war in a mostly uplifting way: seeing 'our brave boys' waving from a ship as they sail off to fight, all smiling, happy and heroic.

If there's a downside, as during the evacuation of Dunkirk in 1940, the newsreel focuses on the courageous rescue of so many men as they are forced to retreat from France. Film of London in the

Did You Know?

Margaret Mitchell, author of the novel *Gone with the Wind*, originally called her feisty heroine 'Pansy', instead of Scarlett. I think she was right to change it.

Pathé News logo

Blitz tells of the bravery shown by those who have been bombed out of their homes and you'll see Churchill or King George and Queen Elizabeth visiting Londoners, all smiling as they bow or curtsy among the rubble.

Then there will be the 'B' film, perhaps with live music playing while the projectionist changes the reel of film. My mum used to play the organ at one local cinema without music scores, playing requests shouted out by the audience. She knew all the 'hits' of the day. The 'B' film is usually without the current 'stars', more cheaply made but often a great story and usually full length. This is followed by an interval while usherettes stand in the aisles selling cigarettes and sweets from their trays. Smoking is allowed in cinemas, as it is in pubs, restaurants, theatres, hotels, shops and on public transport, so you'll have to get used to watching the screen through a haze of smoke, unfortunately.

The show resumes with advertisements and short government information films giving hints on ration book cookery, warning of 'Loose talk costs lives', 'Save your paper' and other such topics, followed by trailers for next week's films. And now, at last, the main feature begins: the 'A' film you've been waiting for. Not bad for a shilling and you get an entire afternoon or evening of entertainment. No wonder cinemas attract audiences of 25–30 million *every week!*

Theatre

In London, the Windmill Theatre remains open throughout, no matter that it suffers bomb damage and close calls, the show must go on. Showgirl Valerie Hudson does her bit, becoming an air-raid warden but, when her duties clash, the stage comes first and she swaps her uniform for her flamboyant dancer's costume. Keeping up public morale is more important.

Pamela Gibson, who goes on to work at Bletchley Park, being a fluent speaker of German, is an actress at heart. She is working at the Mercury Theatre when war is declared and the venue closes, putting her out of a job. She becomes a Red Cross nurse but as soon as the theatres reopen, Pam is ready to go on stage. She recalls one hair-raising experience:

> I was in Birmingham during the Blitz. I remember seeing the flames, it was quite alarming. I was in a hostel with a troupe of Polish dancers from the Prince of Wales Theatre. There was a big air raid and we all went down to the cellar. They all seemed to be absolutely hysterical, I felt terribly grown up and English.

She then notes:

> I now think people who are unafraid are very ignorant and stupid.[2]

Pam also serves in the Entertainments National Services Association (ENSA), putting on shows for servicemen and women, raising their spirits, before being seconded to Bletchley as a translator.

Wireless

With travel restrictions in force, you may have to make do with home entertainment and this is likely to include listening to the wireless (radio). Wireless was promoted as a recent invention in communication by the forces in the Great War and between the wars its possibilities as a public service were realised when the British Broadcasting Corporation (the BBC) began broadcasting in November 1922. By 1939, 9 million households have bought a licence to listen to the programmes, all publicised in the dedicated magazine, the *Radio Times*, which sells a million copies a week.

A wireless costs between £11 10s for a 'Table Standard' model to a free-standing 'Radiogram' at £26 – made by Murphy Ltd in Hertfordshire – but an 'Economy' model which runs on a battery costs only £7 15s, although the battery costs extra.[3] This may be a wise buy in case you want to take it with you to the air-raid shelter or if bombs destroy the power lines, leaving you without electricity.

When war is declared, some in the government believe the BBC should cease broadcasting for the duration but it's realised that the wireless is vital for keeping the public fully informed and up to date with the news as well as providing morale-raising entertainment. On 1 September 1939, the National Service is renamed the Home Service and the Forces Service is set up and becomes popular with everyone. But the *Radio Times* is reduced to twenty pages and its glossy, colourful covers are no more, reduced to just two colours, becoming monochrome later on.

Popular wireless programmes include *Music While You Work*, aimed at factory workers and housewives, playing a variety of light music. *Workers' Playtime* is a morale-booster broadcast at lunchtime three days a week from a different works canteen 'somewhere in Britain'. Big dance bands with their conductors, like Billy Cotton

Did You Know?

Television sets did exist and programmes were broadcast but only in the London area from November 1936 – and not on Sundays. Small sets cost less than £30 but a posh one over £100. By 1939, around 20,000 sets were in use. However, TV broadcasts were suspended on 1 September 1939 and didn't begin again until June 1946, so you couldn't watch television in Britain during the war.

and Victor Sylvester, being the celebrities of the day, often have their own shows and include famous singers, such as Gracie Fields and Vera Lynn.

Of course, the best way to cheer people is to make them laugh and there is a good selection of music hall variety shows on the wireless, such as *Happidrome* and *Garrison Theatre*, as well as comedy programmes. On Saturdays, you can listen to *Bandwagon* with the popular comedians Arthur Askey and Richard Murdoch, though their style of humour is an 'acquired taste' for our twentieth-century ears; their jokes are definitely not PC.

Perhaps *ITMA – It's That Man Again* – will appeal to you, with Tommy Handley running the imaginary Ministry of Aggravation and Mystery, poking satirical fun at the British bureaucracy with its endless forms, red tape and restrictions. It inspires comic-strip cartoons too. Or what about listening in to the *Brains Trust* in which a panel of 'brainy' people discuss topics submitted by the public? Sounds a bit dry, I know, but it's a popular programme with listeners throughout the war.

Other programmes are in formats familiar to you such as dramas, some plays being written especially for the wireless. The *Paul Temple* series features occasionally throughout the war. Begun in 1938, these 'whodunits' continue until the 1960s, often broadcast as a serial of six to eight half-hour programmes for each story, featuring Temple, a novelist with a nose for solving crime, and his wife.

Of course, the most important programmes are the News Bulletins and newsreaders become household names, their voices as familiar as family members. Alvar Lidell is 'the voice' of the wartime BBC, announcing all the biggest and most important events. He continues reading the news for decades and I clearly recall the sound of 'This is Alvar Lidell with the one o'clock news', although I always misheard his name as 'Have-a-little', which quite mystified me as a toddler.

One word of caution, concerning what you'll hear on the wireless: beware of Lord Haw-Haw. That's the nickname given to William Joyce. Joyce was born in New York before his parents brought him to Ireland and then to England. He became a fascist in the 1930s and went to Germany just prior to war being declared. For the first eight months of the war, before hostilities begin in earnest, Joyce broadcasts on German radio from Hamburg to the people of Britain at 9.15 each evening. Putting on a posh English accent and being quite witty, he is popular with listeners, much to the government's and the BBC's concern. The trouble is all to do with propaganda. Joyce is only telling listeners what the Germans wish them to hear but in an appealing way. But the BBC News Bulletins are, likewise, being economical with the truth about what is really happening across Europe in these early days and listeners say that comparing what is said by Lord Haw-Haw to what the BBC is telling them is most likely nearer the truth.

Eventually, Joyce's wittiness fades into dullness. Listeners grow tired of hearing how Britain is doomed and should surrender to German might. Their fighting spirit cannot be broken so easily but Lord Haw-Haw goes on broadcasting throughout the war, still insisting we should surrender on the very day that Hitler commits suicide in May 1945. William Joyce is taken prisoner and brought back to England, where he stands trial and is hanged for treason.

Newspapers, magazines and books

Along with so much else, paper is rationed and newspapers are reduced in size – down to eight pages in many cases, although

The Times usually manages ten and the *Daily Express* as many as twenty-four until rationing hits harder in mid-1940. As with the wireless, the war dominates the news, always attempting to put a positive spin on events. As well as sports reports and film and theatre reviews, just like cinema programmes, newspapers feature helpful hints to deal with rationing, the latest government restrictions and any new changes to your allowances.

Magazines are thinner and gone are the glossy coloured images but here too is advice for coping on the Home Front, how to save fuel, recycle waste paper and metal, and instructions for emergency DIY jobs, such as fixing a leaky tap or mending a fuse. The advertisements are different from what you expect: they no longer exhort the reader to 'buy now' but instead simply remind them that their product, though out of stock for the war, will be back on the shelves as soon as the war ends, better than ever.

Books are also affected by restrictions. Photographic covers are banned and colours limited by War Economy Standard Book Production regulations of 1942. Font size is reduced, the number of words per page increased and as few pages left blank as possible, all on poorer quality paper. This makes for difficult reading what with the use of lower-wattage light bulbs and the blackout. Despite the likelihood of eyestrain, reading books is more popular than it ever was, something to occupy your mind in the air-raid shelter, to whisk you away on the wings of imagination to happier times, perhaps. People share books around but it's reckoned that the cheap paper of a paperback edition can only withstand about twenty readings.

While St Paul's Cathedral in London is famous for surviving the Blitz, what is less well known is that the cathedral sits at the heart of the city's book publishing businesses – as it had done since medieval times – and these are not so fortunate. On 29 December 1940, in what becomes known as the Second Great Fire of London, over five million books go up in flames as the warehouses are bombed and numerous publishing companies are destroyed forever. As *The Bookseller* magazine notes dismally on 1 January 1941, 'It was a crematorium for books.' Connie Miles, who has connections to the London publishing houses, laments the unparalleled loss to literature in her diary and is devastated when she visits her previous haunts in Paternoster Row, just north of the cathedral, for the first time on Thursday, 17 April 1941, four months after the Great Fire. She writes:

> A barrier and a shambles that was the Row, extending far back into a kind of square: all rubbish, planks leaning on bricks, dust, ruin. Where are the lost manuscripts; where the writers' broken hopes?[4]

But Connie also writes on Sunday, 22 September 1940, at the height of the Blitz:

> Women, it is said in London, choose red frocks, hats, coats and flowers after air raids, a device to keep up the spirits.[5]

Celebrations

So, on a brighter, morale-boosting note, let's look at how you might make the most of any reason to celebrate, despite the austerity of rationing, blackout restrictions and, most disappointing, the absence of loved ones.

Christmas

Here is another entry from Connie Miles's diary for Christmas Day 1940:

> I had a marvellous surprise from Harry [her elder son, who was invalided out of the army with a bone disease, had recently sailed for Rhodesia]. It appears he gave Miss Scott, a neighbour, some money to buy me 'white wine and biscuits'. The gift was so magnificent that a

> chocolate cake from Fullers was included and a tin of shortbread from Harrods. … This delighted me so much and took away the loneliness a bit. Went to church and observed that all the priceless old glass has at last been removed and replaced by plain glass.[6]

The following year, on Sunday, 21 December 1941, she tells this lovely story:

> Bey, a friend, told me some touching details of the house full of Czech refugees she looks after. There are some small children who attend school and already have acquired more English than their parents. One child wrote a letter to Santa Claus, asking for certain delectable expensive toys. The poor father, unable to buy them, wrote a letter back from Santa, explaining that there was a war on. The child read it thoughtfully, accepted the reply and only said, 'Santa Claus has made a mistake in his English'.[7]

From the first wartime Christmas of 1939, there are alternative views on buying gifts. The Chancellor of the Exchequer, Sir John Simon, says that money mustn't be 'wasted' on Christmas presents but others insist that this is not only good for morale but patriotic because purchase tax, paid when buying gifts, goes straight into the Exchequer to help the war effort. Some anonymous economist, with no thought for the consequences, reckons the war could be financed entirely through indirect taxation if every adult 'smokes two packets of cigarettes and drinks half a bottle of whisky a day!'[8]

In the UK, the king's, or queen's, Christmas speech to the Empire (or Commonwealth) has become a tradition. It was begun as a wireless broadcast first made by King George V in 1932 and each Christmas following until 1935. In 1936, the new king, Edward VIII, had recently made his abdication speech in mid-December, so there was no Christmas message to the nation and Empire. Now George VI was king and he dreaded making speeches because of his stammer but gave it a go in 1937, only to decide against a repeat performance in 1938. However, in 1939, now we are at war, a Christmas speech by the king would be a great morale-booster and George braces himself.

At 3.00 pm on Christmas Day, after everyone has finished eating dinner, among a full schedule of festive BBC programmes, King George makes a brief but inspiring speech to the Empire about 'struggling on, undaunted', ending: 'May that Almighty Hand [God] guide and uphold us all.' Once the speech concludes, programmes are suspended for a five-minute interval so listeners can digest the words, drinking a toast to His Majesty. Finishing off the last of your Christmas pudding while the king is speaking is a terrible breach of good manners. In fact, many of those in uniform stand to attention throughout the speech. Perhaps it's fortunate that it's brief.

Then programmes resume with an hour of Christmas music, followed by an international family quiz with soldiers in France competing against their loved ones back home with a spelling competition, general knowledge questions and a game of 'passing the message', which we call Chinese Whispers. In fact, the programme schedule includes the whole nation and beyond, broadcasting throughout the Empire and with input from such places as the Sailors' Mission in Swansea, the Foden Motor Works Band, a Christmas Service and an ENSA variety show from 'somewhere in France', a link-up between evacuees in a Gloucestershire village and their parents at home in Stepney, London and links to other festive celebrations going on in a pill-box fort near the front line, an army concert and a children's hospital ward. The BBC certainly tries to make this Christmas as inclusive as possible.

It can't be Christmas without presents but as the war continues, toy manufacturers are making munitions instead and toys are regarded as luxury items. The few that are available, including second-hand ones, are too expensive for ordinary people to buy. The answer is to make your own gifts. If you can knit, sew or glue or do a bit of carpentry,

Did You Know?

King George VI gave his Christmas speech dressed in full naval uniform as Admiral of the Fleet with gold braid up to the elbows, even though only the radio sound crew would see him. He could have made the broadcast in his pyjamas but I suppose the royals had to keep up standards and perhaps the uniform gave him the much-needed confidence he required for public speaking.

there's no end of things you can invent. Or, if you need a bit of help, pre-Christmas magazines are full of ideas, knitting patterns for toys and sewing patterns for all kinds of novelties.

Guider magazine for Girl Guides advises you to collect fabric scraps to make soft toys, suggesting grey flannel for elephants – but why not other, brighter colours? – old tweed for horses and felt or velour for rabbits. Craft Council patterns and instructions for sewing these animals cost 1s. The same magazine tells you how to make gas-mask cases from pretty scraps of material or simply to glue bright fabric pieces onto the standard-issue cardboard box.

If you're handy with hammer and nails, a young lad's dream could be a homemade go-kart, though these have various names across Britain. It's a wooden box mounted on a plank with old pram wheels and steered with a length of string. Marvellous fun.

Top Tip

If glue can't be obtained, a runny mix of flour and water will do the job as paste. Also, if you have unravelled an old cardigan to reuse the wool to knit Christmassy bed-socks or suchlike and the wool is too kinked to work with, wind the wool tightly around a glass bottle, fill the bottle with hot water and leave it to cool. By the time the water is cold, your wool should be straight as new.

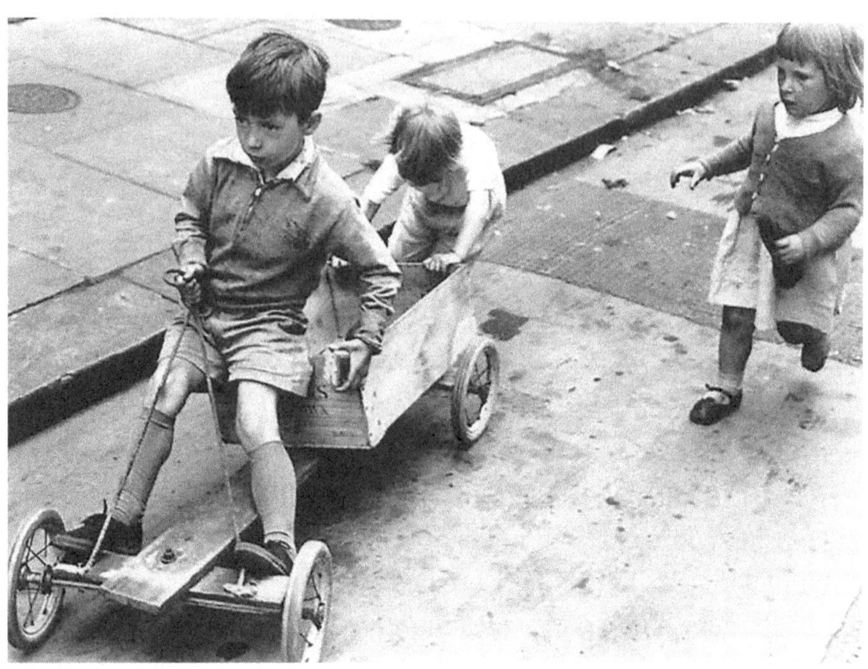

A boy's dream Christmas gift: a go-kart, box-cart, trolley, bogey or gooby (in Wales). Echo Ireland

By Christmas 1940, rationing has become a way of life, but the government does its bit to cheer up the festive season with a special treat for all. In the week leading up to Christmas Day, the tea ration is doubled from 2 ozs to 4 ozs per person and the sugar allowance is raised from 8 ozs to 12 ozs per person so cakes, marzipan and icing can be made. But it's back to normal after Boxing Day.

There are recipes for 'mock' turkey – actually stuffed rabbit – and how to make and decorate a cake in the shape of an Anderson shelter.

Or you could bake 'fake' sausage rolls using potato pastry wrapped around a mashed mixture of baked beans and a quarter-tin of American Spam. Some of that extra sugar ration could make toffee-coated nuts as gifts for friends. Shell cobnuts, hazel nuts or filberts – all homegrown nuts – and put them on a baking sheet in a warm oven. Heat them a little until you can rub off the brown skins.

A Christmas cake in the shape of an Anderson shelter. World War II House, Sittingbourne, GRM

Make the toffee mixture with 4 ozs sugar, ½ oz margarine, a pinch of cream of tartar and 2½ tablespoons of water. Dissolve the sugar in the water; add the margarine and cream of tartar. Bring to the boil and cook until a little dropped in cold water turns brittle. Use a fork to dip each nut into the hot toffee then let them cool on waxed paper until the toffee sets. Pack into little decorated bags and there you have the perfect Christmas treats.

Paper chains made with strips of newspaper glued into links and tree decorations are also homemade. Little boxes made from wallpaper cut-offs are hung from the Christmas tree, looking very festive, though probably empty, unless you've made extra toffee-coated nuts.

Did You Know?

In England, 'Banns of Marriage' must be read out on three consecutive Sundays in the couple's parish church (or churches, if they live in different parishes) or displayed for three weeks in the local Registry Office, if it's a civil marriage, before the wedding day. This allows anyone who objects to the union, such as another spouse (!), to come forward. But if there are only a few days to set up the arrangements and no time for banns, a special licence must be obtained from the bishop of the diocese.

Weddings

It may seem strange but, during the war, Christmas is often the time for weddings. This is because the forces try to arrange leave for as many serving men as possible, if they're stationed in Britain, to be with their families. With loved ones briefly reunited, it's a good time to get married, but this may mean arrangements have to be made at very short notice.

Joyce Thomas and Albert 'Lofty' Botting are to be wed at short notice, not at Christmas but on Wednesday, 26 May 1943. Let's ask them how they're managing the arrangements:

'Congratulations to you both. So, tomorrow is the big day?'

'Yes, and we're so excited about it, aren't we, Lofty? It's been such a rush. Yesterday, we had to see the Bishop of Rochester to get a special licence. I thought we would talk to the bishop himself but his secretary did it all but he was very nice, wasn't he, Lofty? I expect the bishop's a very busy man.'

'How long have you had to plan the wedding?'

'Just six days, then it's the wedding tomorrow, then a day's honeymoon and Lofty's special leave ends on Friday. I didn't know anything about it until last Thursday when he turned up on the doorstep and said, "What do you think about getting married next week, Joy?" I didn't even know he was coming on leave. Of course, I said yes. After all, we've been engaged for nearly a year. See my engagement ring? It's platinum with little diamonds…'

'It's very pretty, Joyce. What will you wear tomorrow?'

'A proper wedding dress and veil, though the shoes are a problem. I'm borrowing my cousin Peggy's dress. She married Len in the summer before the war. And she's going to wear the lilac bridesmaid's dress her sister Doris wore that day and be my matron-of-honour. Good thing we're all about the same size but I can't wear her white shoes as she's got such small feet but a neighbour says she's got some white sandals in my size that I can borrow.'

'What about flowers?'

'Oh, Mr Hepton across the road grows carnations and, luckily, he hasn't dug them all up to grow potatoes. He says they should make a grand bouquet for me, along with some fern.'

'And the cake?'

'Mum's had a word with the aunts: all five of them live in this road, you know, all the neighbours and friends in Nelson Road have donated ingredients for the cake. Mum baked it yesterday. No marzipan or icing, though, but Mrs Ventham gave us some glacé cherries and a bottle of sherry she was saving for a special occasion.'

'What of the guests? Has there been time to invite them?'

'Well, all my aunts are coming: Em and Uncle George, May and Uncle Arthur (Peggy's parents), Ellen and Uncle Lowell, Hilda and Ethel, Uncle Ab and Uncle Wally and any cousins who can. I hoped my brother, Sid, would give me away but he's in North Africa somewhere, so Uncle Arthur Deadman, Mum's eldest brother, is going to do it.'

'What about your relatives, Lofty?'

'My Aunt Kit is coming from Maidstone on the train.'

'Lofty was an orphan so his aunt is his only family, apart from his brothers. But Harry's in a submarine and Joe's a drunk, so he's not invited.'

'They don't want to know that, Joy, love. And don't forget Jack, my best man.'

'Lofty, why did you get this special leave to get married?'

'I can't tell you much but I'm going to a new ship in Scotland. That's all I can say. But now we have to go and collect Joy's wedding ring.'

'And see the parson at All Saints, Lofty, don't forget... and the photographer. Oh, I'm so nervous...'

'Good luck for tomorrow and I wish you a happy life together.'[9]

Although icing is banned on wedding cakes, there is a small extra food allowance which you can apply for, giving details of how many guests are coming. I don't know where my parents held the reception, perhaps at Joyce's home at 87 Nelson Road, but having everyone

Joyce and Albert Botting's wedding photo taken at All Saints Church, Northfleet, Kent, 26 May 1943. Note that Lofty is wearing a white 'dicky' bow on his naval uniform, only ever worn by the bridegroom on the wedding day. Amy Thomas, the bride's mother, is the woman to the right in the pale dress. Aunt Kit is far left. Uncle Arthur stands between Amy and Peggy, the matron-of-honour. Author's own photograph

helping with the catering, offering whatever they can, is often how it's done. Not all wartime brides can borrow a traditional wedding dress, as Joyce does, and a day dress or a two-piece and a hat, all of which can be worn on other occasions, are the choice of many women for their 'Big Day'. Some even wear uniform.

Once married, wives can access their husband's pay if he is serving in the forces by means of a pay-book which they take to the Post Office once a week to have it stamped and money is handed over.[10] They may also be entitled to a widow's pension if the worst happens.

Keeping up morale

In her diary, on Sunday, 23 March 1941, Connie Miles has this to say:

> At supper of shredded cabbage and carrots, Robin and I discussed the mystery of the great London air raids – the endurance and indifference to them displayed by so many people we know who we should have imagined would have simply crumpled up and fled … Yet they stick it week after week and hardly mention it.[11]

She tells of bombed-out people at a Rest Centre:

> One old chap, quite bald, had soot completely over his pate. He submitted to a child trying to write 'Grandad' on his head with laughter. Wonderful London![12]

Anything you can do to raise morale will be appreciated but there are more practical ways to help with the war effort, as we'll see in the next chapter.

Chapter 8

How Could I Do My Bit to Support the War Effort?

Recycling

If you believe that recycling is a twenty-first century idea, think again. During the war just about everything is recycled, from tea leaves (see Chapter 2) to iron railings and *waste not, want not* becomes the motto of the times. It goes without saying that saving fuel is a top priority but, from July 1940, people are encouraged to donate any pots and pans they can manage without to make plane fuselages, bayonets and so on, recycle waste paper and cardboard, rubber and even meat fat and bones![1]

The paper is used to insulate air-raid shelters or re-pulped and made into 'new' paper for all those millions of government forms, maps and ration books. It's also used in the munitions industry to make mortar bomb carriers and washers for the shells. Over 56 million old books are sent for recycling but 6 million, those reckoned to be too valuable, are saved for posterity and almost as many of the more popular titles are sent to troops abroad for light reading.

Though the technology of recycling is quite basic, since almost everything is made from natural materials, it can be reused in surprising ways. After Japan enters the war in December 1941, Britain is cut off from her usual Malaysian rubber supplies, so all spare rubber is wanted to produce tyres, gas masks, emergency escape dinghies, barrage balloons and soles for troops' boots. Only Bakelite objects – the first plastic – used for telephone handsets, the outer casing of wireless and TV sets, cannot be recycled.

Rags are collected up and recycled as blankets and bandages. Cooking fat from roasting meat can be turned into glycerine to make explosives, as can the bones, which are also used to make glue used in plane construction and fertiliser for food production. When you have set aside quite a lot of stuff for recycling, some local councils provide signs for you to put outside your door so the collectors know where to stop with their van. Other councils expect you to bring what you save to the recycling centres. Either way, you are 'doing your bit' to aid the war effort.

In a wireless broadcast in July 1940, the Minister of Supply, Herbert Morrison – after whom the Morrison indoor air-raid shelter is named – asked that: 'People start now and save their paper, bones and scrap metal. In that way, we shall build up a great reserve of raw materials ready to be transformed into war materials.' The response is incredible. People of all ages turn up at collection points to hand over aluminium pots and pans for salvage and soon get used to separating rubbish into boxes for glass, paper, metal, rubber and rags. By 1942, 60 per cent of new paper is being made from recycled waste paper and card from old newspapers, and shop packaging although, later in the war, most packaging of shop-bought goods is banned.

In April 1941, following the success of a plea for aluminium for aircraft production the previous summer, the Ministry of Supply announced the great need of 'the type of scrap metal which may be obtained from railings and which has a special value in the manufacture of ships' cables, chains and other fittings'. In September, local authorities are ordered to carry out surveys to determine any railings in their area which could be reckoned 'unnecessary'. Owners of such railings have only a fortnight to appeal against their removal on artistic, historic or safety grounds. This new project is designed to raise 500,000 tons of scrap – enough to fit out 300 destroyers. The removal of the railings outside Buckingham Palace is given a lot of publicity, as is that of the three miles of railings – 1,000 tons – taken from Hyde Park in Central London. By March 1942, London is collecting 5,000 tons of iron railings and gates from 45,000 properties each week.[2]

By the end of the campaign in September 1944, over one million tons of railings have been collected. As a propaganda and morale exercise, it's a brilliant success but far more iron is acquired than can be used.[3]

From February 1942, you can volunteer as a nationwide Salvage Steward and wear a red badge as a part-time collector, appointed by the local council, or a blue badge for those in shops and offices and a green badge if you're salvaging stuff from local factories. The Boy Scouts and Girl Guides are helping with collection throughout the war and the WVS organises children to work as Junior Salvage Stewards, known as 'Cogs'. They have their own anthem: 'There'll Always Be a Dustbin', sung to the tune of 'There'll Always Be an England'.

Warship Weeks

The introduction of the scrap iron campaign coincides with the start of a new savings scheme: Warship Weeks. Between October 1941 and the end of March 1942, Warship Weeks are organised by the National War Savings Committee, with the support of the Admiralty, in cities, towns and villages throughout Britain. The intention is to raise a sum of money by investment or deposit in all types of war savings, enough to cover the cost of building one of His Majesty's ships, ranging from the smallest to the largest vessels. Fund-raising targets are set according to the size of the community, so a city might be asked to raise £2+ million to adopt an aircraft carrier while a village has a target of £25,000 to sponsor a motor torpedo boat (MTB). Sometimes, small villages club together to raise enough for a bigger ship and targets are usually exceeded. The district receives a plaque and scroll naming the vessel they have adopted and presented, if possible, by the commanding officer. Before Warship Weeks are set up officially, some schools and local societies have already had the idea, as this poignant newspaper article tells:

> Evening Despatch, Wednesday 10 July 1940 – Mothers Union Loses Adopted Destroyer: News of the sinking of the destroyer *Whirlwind* has been received with deep regret at Bridgnorth, where St. Leonard's Mother's Union six months ago adopted *Whirlwind.* At that time it's understood that St. Leonard's Mother's Union was the first organisation of its kind to adopt a destroyer. During the intervening period monthly consignments of comforts have been despatched, and as recently as last Saturday two parcels were sent.

HMS *Whirlwind* is torpedoed and sunk on 5 July 1940 with the loss of fifty-seven men: half her crew, just six months after she was adopted.[4]

Some districts keep in touch, exchanging gifts, letters and visits from crew members of their adopted ship for years beyond the war. Others don't.

You can help by buying Government Bonds, National Savings Certificates or putting a few shillings into a Post Office Savings Bank account. You are only lending the money to the government and you'll receive 2½–3 per cent interest on your savings. In total, more than £955.5 million is raised during Warship Weeks, sponsoring four aircraft carriers, eight battleships, twenty-five submarines, forty-nine cruisers, 301 destroyers, 154 corvettes and frigates, 288 minesweepers and 339 MTBs, motor gunboats (MGBs), launches, sloops and smaller coastal vessels.

Other than Warship Weeks, there is War Weapons Week to replace equipment lost at Dunkirk and the Buy Your Own Spitfire campaign held in 1940 during the Battle of Britain to replace lost fighter planes. In 1941, it's Tanks for Attack Week; 1943 sees Wings for Victory Week to buy bombers and Salute the Soldier Week in 1944. This last campaign begins with a large military parade in Trafalgar Square in London. It aims to raise money for field hospitals, medical equipment and supplies and is very successful, bringing in £628,021,000 – almost

HMS *Chanticleer*, a modified Black Swan-class sloop, was launched on 24 September 1941. She was adopted by the author's hometown of Gravesend in Kent after a successful Warship Week in March 1942. IWM & Wikicommons

£35 billion in 2025. All these campaigns raise money by means of the National Savings Scheme as with Warship Weeks.

Make Do and Mend

This is everyone's motto and refers to everything from saving fuel to darning socks. The Make Do and Mend campaign is given official support by the Board of Trade in 1942, trying to make people think differently about the clothes they wear and everyday items they use: that you cannot buy new when the old wears out. You must repair, fix and make things last.

If you don't know how to mend a hole in a garment, from the summer of 1942, there are numerous leaflets produced by the Board of Trade under the pseudonym of Mrs Sew-and-Sew with clear instructions on how to darn, patch and repair just about anything. The WI and the WVS run classes where you can learn these useful skills. According to the *Home Companion* magazine in July 1943, 'Patched elbows these days are no disgrace', in fact, they're now a fashion statement in a contrasting colour or pattern, showing that you're 'doing your bit' to help the war effort.

Because nobody knows how long the war and the shortages will continue, your clothes, bed linens and blackout curtains may need to last years. Mrs Sew-and-Sew has leaflets full of tips on how to make such things last longer by lining them before they wear into holes, how to guard against moths and the best ways of washing and caring for different fabrics.

Apart from needlework, there are leaflets on DIY with instructions on how to change a washer on a leaky tap, mend a fuse, unblock a sink waste, put a new pane of glass in a window and solder a saucepan. This selection of fix-its comes from a leaflet titled 'Simple jobs boys can do themselves – and so help win the war'. And, of course, there's a similar leaflet for girls which tells you how to care for brushes so they last longer, from toothbrushes to scrubbing brushes, making polishing pads out of leather scraps, mending lace or net curtains – which are a good idea to guard against glass splinters from windows in an air raid – tips on ironing and fixing a stuck drawer using a chisel and candle wax.

A most important Ministry of Home Security Leaflet, issued in December 1940 – a bit too late for some, unfortunately – has full instructions on how to plan for the possibility of your home being damaged or destroyed in an air raid. 'There is a great deal of help ready for you, if you have suffered in the national interest as well as in your own fight against Hitler', the leaflet says, making your loss sound like a patriotic gesture instead of a very real devastating calamity. It also suggests that you should make arrangements to stay with friends or family if this happens or for them to come to you, if they suffer the same, and perhaps exchange small bags of a few clothes and necessities beforehand, just in case. The government will pay the hosts 5 shillings per adult per week and 3 shillings per child. It's important to make sure both the authorities and any relatives know of your change of address so you can be accounted for as a survivor and receive any assistance you need.

If you have nobody with whom you can stay and, as a recent visitor, this may well be so, there are Rest Centres where you will be given food and shelter and treated for shock and minor injuries, if necessary. Officers at the centre will help you get money, clothes, a new ration book and ID card and find somewhere for you to stay with a free travel voucher to get you there, if required. Hopefully, your home is only damaged and can be made safe and fit to live in again and you can receive compensation to pay for repairs, if you own the property, or the landlord will get the money, if you rent it.

If your home is liveable but the gas and electricity supplies have been damaged by air raids or shut down for safety reasons, you are entitled to use a Community Kitchen, which will provide you with meals: 4d–6d for a main dish, 2d–3d for a dessert, 1d for a cup of tea and children's portions are half price.

Should the worst happen and you are injured and cannot work, you'll receive a war-injury allowance, providing you fill out the appropriate forms, of course. If the injury is serious and long term, you can be considered for a disability pension. But that's not going to happen, is it? You made this time-travelling journey for fun, so how can you 'do your bit' in other ways?

Avoid loose talk

Or 'keep mum', as the saying goes, meaning 'keep silent'. At least this way of helping the war effort doesn't require any manual skills or cost money and it doesn't need coupons. But talking too freely *is* rationed. The government is paranoid about enemy spies lurking everywhere: in the pub, in the shopping queue, in the seat behind you on the bus, overhearing your conversation. As we heard previously, many workers have signed the Official Secrets Act, whether at the top-secret Station X at Bletchley Park, manufacturing armaments or aeroplane parts, growing camomile to disguise aerodrome runways or joining the services. But everyone is implored to say nothing that may help the enemy and it's hard to tell what information might be of use to a foreign spy.

You'll see 'Keep Mum' posters everywhere, reminding you not to talk to a neighbour about the letter you received from a friend stationed with the army in North Africa or at an RAF aerodrome in Lincolnshire, in case someone is 'listening in'. Or could your neighbour be the spy? Oh dear, such thoughts breed suspicion and paranoia but do think before you speak. The British are renowned for discussing the weather as their main topic of conversation and now you can understand why: because it's a safe subject.

This 'Keep Mum' poster reminds people that anyone, even this glamorous woman, could be a spy. TNA

Did You Know?

Seamen's cap bands now only carry the letters 'HMS' – His Majesty's Ship – and no longer the name of the ship. This is so that enemy spies, seeing a sailor on shore, won't know which naval vessel is in port. It's even 'Top Secret' how many cups of tea are drunk by the Civil Servants in Whitehall's government departments.

Any letters you do receive, especially from anyone in the armed forces abroad, will have been read by a censor before it reaches you. It may have been redacted with dates, names, places and anything else which might be important made illegible. This could make it a boring and nonsensical letter: 'On … I went with … to … We had a great time.' But at least you'll know they're all right.

However, ordinary mail isn't censored, so be careful how and where you keep letters that contain important information, like this sad titbit written to Connie Miles from her friend Phyllis Hazeldine on Thursday, 16 July 1942:

> I have been in awful trouble since last I wrote, having lost my beloved little sergeant-pilot son. He and the whole four boys of his crew never returned from air operations over Emden on the night of 26 June and nothing has been heard of them since. It nearly killed me, all the more as the suspense was terrible, waiting and hoping against hope.[5]

Hitler could make great propaganda out of this mother's story of loss.

Holidays at home

Before this war began, on the whole, only the rich could afford foreign holidays. For the average British family, the traditional summer holiday meant a trip to the seaside, maybe camping, staying in bed-and-breakfast accommodation or a cheap hotel. But the war has ended that in so many ways: petrol rationing and limited travel on public transport make it difficult to journey any distance except for official purposes. Besides, with beaches covered in barbed wire and 'Entry Forbidden: Mines!' signs all along our coasts, the seaside is out of bounds. By 1940, annual leave is cancelled in factories as there's no time off from the war effort when it's a matter of national survival.

But people aren't machines and an occasional break from work is vital for moral and relief of stress. By 1942, the government realises this and invents the Stay-at-Home-Holiday Scheme, encouraging factories to give the workforce a week's leave to spend at home. They even issue a leaflet, 'Suggested Menus for Holidays at Home', giving snack and picnic recipes which are supposed to give the housewife a bit of a rest from cooking too.

Here is a taster of what the leaflet suggests for Monday's picnic lunch and hot supper – the washing-up rota is a great idea:

Lunch – sandwiches made with pilchard and cabbage spread*, watercress, shredded cabbage heart or lettuce, homemade salad dressing, homemade fairy sponge cakes [baked on Sunday].

Supper – cold meat left over from the Sunday roast, new potatoes with peas, beans or cabbage. Dessert – poor knight's fritters. These last are bread and jam sandwiches dipped in a mixture of dried egg in milk. The sandwiches are then fried in hot fat, turning once until golden and crisp. [The fritters would be nice with ice cream, if there is any.]

---

* The spread is made using a 4 oz tin of pilchards in tomato sauce, 4 ozs finely shredded cabbage, 1 tablespoon chopped parsley, 1 tablespoon vinegar, 1 level teaspoon mustard, salt. Mix all ingredients together and beat until smooth. Use as a filling for sandwiches, rolls or savoury scones.

Local councils are encouraged to arrange band concerts in the park and other outdoor entertainments for the stay-at-home holiday makers. But if you cannot bear to stay at home for the one week free of your usual work, you could volunteer to 'Lend a hand on the land', working at an agricultural farm camp for 1 shilling an hour. Although your accommodation will cost 28 shillings, it's described as 'hard work but healthy with good fun in the evenings'.[6] You'll deserve that 'fun' whatever it entails and they say 'a change is as good as a rest'. I hope it is.

The Women's Voluntary Service

If you have time to spare and want to do more to assist those affected by the situation, perhaps you could join the WVS. The Home Office set up the WVS in 1938 to assist in the event of possible future air attacks and by the time war is declared on 3 September 1939, the organisation already has 165,000 members. Their work soon diversifies, helping in all areas of the Home Front. One of their earliest jobs is to assist with the evacuation of 1.5 million mothers and children from large cities to the countryside. They also provide food and clothing for thousands of refugees from occupied Europe who flee to Britain.

When air raids begin, the WVS are to the fore, fully involved in providing support for those whose homes have been bombed, organising Rest Centres, preparing food and ensuring washing facilities and new clothes for bomb victims. Later in the war, they man Incident Inquiry Points, giving information about loved ones, the dead and injured, to relatives and friends. They also support the emergency services, dealing with the effects of the bombing, running mobile canteens for firemen, civil defence and other rescue workers.

The WVS staff hostels, clubs and the 'British Restaurants' (see Chapter 3) and carry out welfare work for troops, including members of the Merchant Navy who receive no pay from the moment their ship

> **Did You Know?**
>
> After the war, the Home Office announced that the WVS should continue for 'possibly two years' but, in fact, it still exists today, providing support in emergencies and carrying out welfare services, particularly for the elderly. In 1966 the organisation was awarded royal status, becoming the Women's Royal Voluntary Service (WRVS).

is sunk and can be left destitute, losing everything despite their loyal service. When American troops arrive in Britain in 1942, the WVS runs 200 'Welcome Clubs' all over the country, attempting to make them feel at home and bring together the GIs and the local civilians. The WVS volunteers are often responsible for setting up and running the recycling campaigns and organising clothing exchanges.

By the end of 1941, the WVS has enrolled its millionth member and many are older women. It gives them a chance to use their skills and abilities, rather than sitting at home, waiting out the war in boredom. Apart from a few admin staff, WVS members aren't paid and have to buy their own uniform of green coats and dresses with burgundy cardigans, green and burgundy scarves, and felt hats, but it's designed by the top London fashion designer, Digby Morton, so it looks good.

The Navy, Army and Air Force Institutes

Or you could volunteer to work for the NAAFI, which was set up in 1920 to sell goods to servicemen and their families and to arrange recreational activities for the armed forces. During the war, the NAAFI grows and by April 1944, its 96,000 personnel are running 10,000 outlets, including 7,000 canteens and 900 mobile shops. It runs club houses and bars, shops, launderettes where you can do your washing, cafés and restaurants on most British military bases

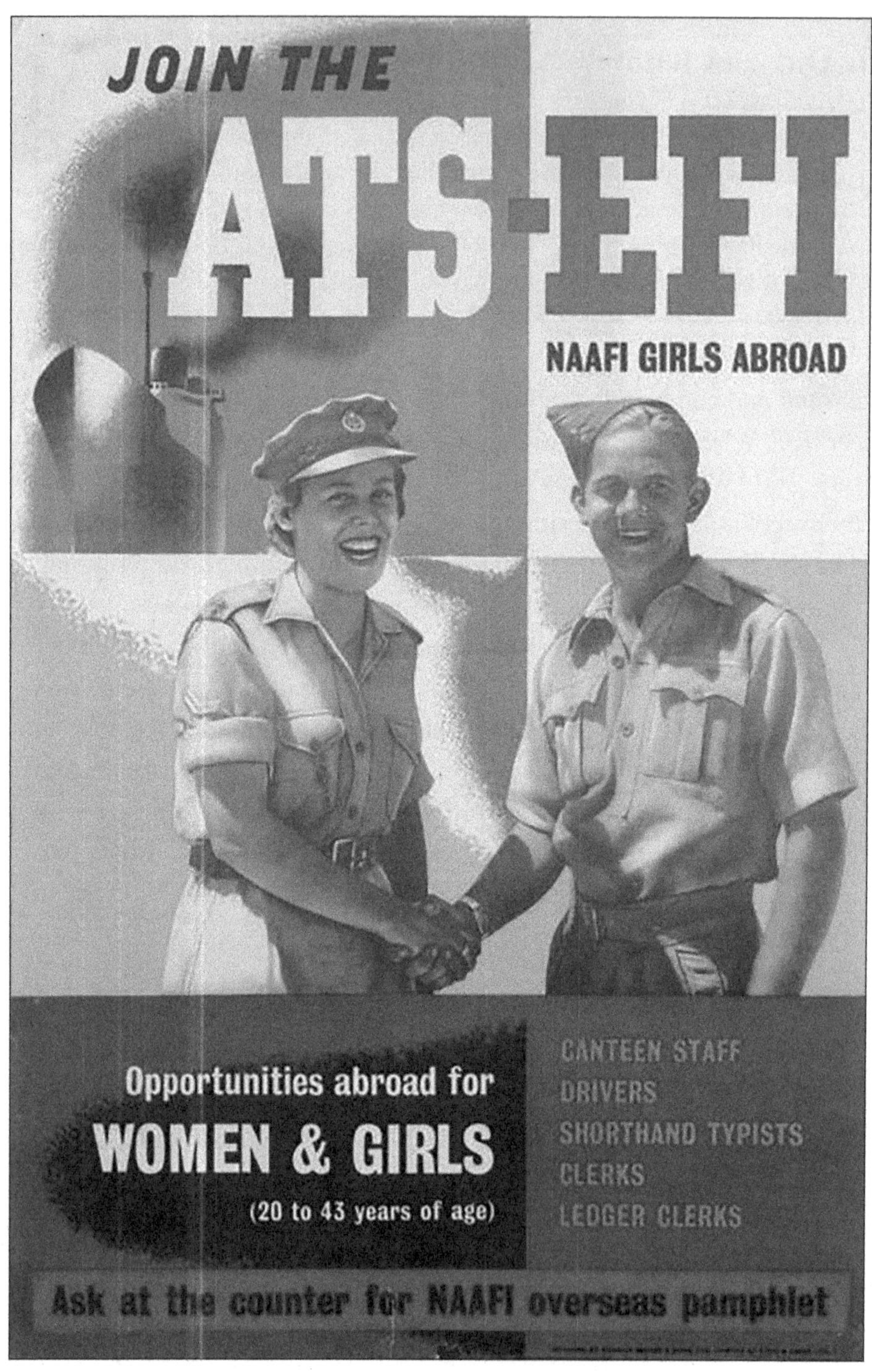

An advertising poster for both NAAFI and EFI volunteers. IWM

Did You Know?

One member of ENSA, Vivienne Fayre, an acrobatic dancer aged 19, is killed in Normandy in January 1945 when the truck carrying stage scenery, in which she was a passenger, drove over a mine. She is buried with full military honours.

and canteens on board Royal Navy vessels. In this last case, members wear naval uniform but remain civilians. NAAFI establishments are for the junior ranks only. No officers allowed. The Expeditionary Forces Institutes (EFI) is the male version of the NAAFI and they, too, are classed as civilians, despite the uniform.

The NAAFI also organises Entertainments National Service Association (ENSA), which provides entertainment for the armed forces with singing stars of the day, like Vera Lynn and Gracie Fields, comedic singer George Formby and actor Noël Coward among the entertainers. Other, less famous members of ENSA, like Terry-Thomas, Peter Sellers, Spike Milligan and Kenneth Connor become well known after the war.

If you enjoy shop-work or catering, or fancy becoming a showgirl, this may be the job for you and a smart ATS khaki uniform is supplied for free.

Other job opportunities for women

Before the war, most women were expected, or even forced in some cases such as the Civil Service, to leave their jobs if they got married, but the war changes that. Now housewives don't have to dedicate themselves to caring for their husbands, homes and families. They can go out and get a useful civilian job which often comes with a uniform, for instance, as conductresses on buses, trams or trolley buses. If you're unfamiliar with what a bus conductress, or 'clippie' does, in this age of pre-paid tickets, travel cards, and so on, she collects your fare for the journey and issues the ticket once you're seated. She can tell you which bus number you'll need if you intend to journey farther on or to a destination other than the one the current bus is heading for, what time the bus will return and – most important in the blackout – when you've reached the stop where you want to disembark if you don't recognise it. Let's ask a clippie on the Sheffield trams about her work:

'Good afternoon, miss. May I ask you about your job?'

'You can but I'm a missus, not a miss. Which stop do you want?'

'Er, where do you suggest? In the city centre, maybe?'

'There's the fish market but you look a bit smart for that. Or the posh shops where the ladies-of-leisure go to buy their twenty-guineas-a-time, non-Utility frocks, perfume and silk stockings and pay by cheque. They expect me to call them "madam". Hard to credit that underneath all that finery they're women just like me. But then I've got the authority of my made-to-measure uniform to impress them.'

'You certainly have. I'll go to the fish market, please.'

'That'll be a tu'penny fare then. I used to be a journalist before I got married, you know. Interesting work that was but I wasn't allowed to carry on once I was wed, though I wanted to.'

'I've only got a sixpence, sorry.'

'Don't matter. I've plenty of pennies for change. They'll be grubby though 'cos they're from this morning's factory workers and school children. My hands go black with the dirt off their money.'

'Are most of your passengers factory workers?'

'First thing in the morning they are. Then come the office workers and shop assistants with clean hands and clean clothes, looking nice. After them, it's the bosses in suits and bowler hats, clean-shaven with crisp white collars. Mind you, they look uncomfortable on a tram, being used to driving to work in their own cars, but the petrol rationing stopped all that. That's why the trams get so busy. Then of course, they all have to go home again: school children first, then office staff and bosses, then shop girls and, finally, the factory workers.'

'It must be a long day for them…'

'And longer still for me! The last tram gets back to the depot at 11o'clock, then I have to do the money and hand it to Mr Jessup to put in the safe. If the cash and ticket sales don't tally up properly, I may not finish 'til after midnight and then I have to walk home through the blackout, praying my boy has had supper and put himself to bed. He's 13, so old enough but all the same… and my poor feet after all that! I've been on the trams since 7 o'clock this morning and it'll be the same t'morrow. I hardly see my lad.'

'You're very busy…'

'That I am and this next stop is the fish market, so off you get.'

'Thank you and goodbye.'[7]

Being a clippie isn't the easy option then but she does get to meet all sorts of people.

The General Post Office

During the war, the General Post Office (GPO) is a stalwart British institution with a reputation for reliability. It has its own Home Guard and Salvage Crews to rescue letters and so on from blown-up post boxes and bomb-damaged post offices and they still aim to deliver all mail delayed by enemy action within forty-eight hours.[8] Connie Miles complains in her diary that the cost of posting a letter has increased to 2½d on 1 May 1940 – 'It seems an enormous sum for a letter', she says. Britain relies on its postmen and postwomen to deliver all those help-the-war-effort leaflets, information letters and bureaucratic red tape promptly and efficiently. The GPO also maintains the telephone system, which is vital to communications. The country cannot function without them.

To help in this mission, Frederick G. Gurr establishes the GPO Rescue and Salvage Squad to rescue mail, money and supplies from post offices bombed in the City of London. Gurr compiles newspaper cuttings and photographs recounting his team's efforts in scrapbooks and is awarded the British Empire Medal by King George VI for his heroism.

In Manchester, the main Post Office is in the Central Exchange Building. One night, during an incendiary bombardment, all the surrounding textile warehouses are an inferno. Despite the Fire Brigade's best efforts, when the water pressure supplying their hoses fails at dawn, the Post Office is surrounded by burning buildings. Although warned by fire-fighters that there is great danger from falling masonry, a postman, Mr Little, and two colleagues make their way through the clouds of smoke and somehow succeed in putting

The GPO Salvage Squad rescues mail from a post box destroyed in the Blitz. www.postalmuseum.org/blog/the-post-office-during-wwii

out the fires inside the Central Exchange, saving the building and all the equipment inside. Mr Little is awarded the George Medal and his colleagues receive the Order of the British Empire for their 'gallantry and for the enterprise displayed by them in saving the building'.[9] It sounds a very hazardous job being a postman or woman but you may feel this could be the way to 'do your bit', if you have courage enough.

The GPO, factories and other important buildings rely on fire-watchers, who stay on the roof during air raids, armed with buckets of water and sand, stirrup-pumps and beaters to put out fires before they can take hold. Many an elderly postmistress finds herself obliged to do this to keep the mail safe.

I feel that we now deserve a little fun to cheer us up. In the next chapter, we'll look at some of the strange, miraculous or simply weird things that are going on in Britain during the Second World War.

Chapter 9

Strange But True

In this chapter, we're going to discover some of the odd facts about what is happening on the Home Front during the war: some of the strange things that it's hoped might aid the war effort or help people cope with problems of everyday life. But let's begin with a group of individuals I haven't mentioned before that is important to us all.

What about our pets?

I'm afraid I have sad news so let's get that out of the way first: at the outbreak of war, many pets are sacrificed. The National Air Raid Precautions Animals Committee (NARPAC) believes that England is home to six to seven million dogs and cats, 56 million poultry, and more than 37 million farm animals: about twice as many domestic animals as there are people. War means the possibility of air raids, rationing and severe food shortages. With these problems in mind, NARPAC issues an advisory pamphlet to animal owners encouraging them to send their animals to the countryside. But if the animals can't be taken into someone else's care, the pamphlet suggests it would be 'kindest to have them destroyed'.

On 3 September 1939, thousands of people do what they think is their duty and take their pets to the local veterinary clinic to have them 'put to sleep'. Vets hate doing this to healthy animals and most of the owners are probably distraught at having their beloved companions put down. But they are sparing their pets the terror of air raids, the privations of no pet food or sharing the most meagre of human rations and the possibility that the loss of their owners in an air raid might leave them to starve. Hundreds of thousands of dogs, cats, birds and small animals are given up in this way.

But not all. Amy Thomas's collie dog, Bruce, hides under the bed during an air raid, refusing to go down to the Anderson shelter in the back garden. His superb canine hearing can tell the difference between friendly and enemy planes and he carries on as normal if the good guys fly overhead. But if Bruce bolts upstairs to hide then Amy knows she just has time to make a flask of tea and get her things together, ready for the shelter, before the siren sounds. Sadly, public shelters and Rest Centres don't permit pets so some people risk the raids to stay at home with their animals.

A man who lives in Shoreditch, East London, sends his wife and children to the safety of the local shelter but he stays home with his cat and pet rabbit, though bombs fall close by. He says, if he left the animals, he wouldn't be able to think about anything else except how the animals were getting on.[1]

And animals return the favour: an Alsatian named Jet is a search-and-rescue dog responsible for saving 150 people during the Blitz. On one occasion, he finds a woman buried in the wreckage of a hotel and sits by her for twelve hours until rescuers dig her out. Jet receives the Dickin Medal in 1945 – the animals' equivalent of Britain's highest award for courage, the Victoria Cross.[2]

But there are difficulties in feeding pets. An advertisement for 'Chappie' dog food in *Illustrated* magazine, dated 5 December 1942,

Top Tip

One suggestion to feed your dog is to make 'Mickey's Dog Biscuits': mix oatmeal porridge with plain flour, ½ lb of each, flavour it with 2 Oxo cubes, (although these are meant to flavour gravy to serve with the Sunday roast) and add ½ pint of hot water. Roll out the dough and cut into rounds with an egg cup. Bake the biscuits for 40 minutes until light brown and hard.

admits that the product is rationed and you 'maybe unable to obtain Chappie at present', but reminds customers that as soon as 'conditions permit … you need never feed [your dog] on anything else'. Spratt's Dog Biscuits advertises, saying 'Try Again for Spratt's – You may be lucky next time'. The RSPCA (Royal Society for the Prevention of Cruelty to Animals) and Bob Martin's (manufacturers of health products and 'conditioning' pills for dogs) publish leaflets on how to feed dogs and cats throughout rationing.

But some dogs have their own ideas, as Connie Miles notes in her diary on 12 July 1940:

> The local bone dump [where bones are collected for recycling] has had to be put on a high pole as the village dogs conceived the idea that we were doing war work for them.[3]

Food for caged birds, such as budgerigars, parrots and canaries, is also in short supply. 'Make your meagre supply of bird seed stretch as far as possible', seems to be the only advice but some garden weeds, such as chickweed, shepherd's purse, dandelions and some thistle seeds heads are excellent bird food.

Cats are reckoned to be able to fend for themselves, catching mice and birds and eating scraps, but Connie Miles continues to pamper her cat, Muff, as much as possible, as she writes in her diary on Monday, 23 December 1940:

> Muff, all soft grey, is settling down on a piece of golden-coloured brocade for the evening. The only food I could get for him today was 'chickens' heads four pence a pound'. No fish, no lights.[4]

An enthusiastic cat-lover, Connie records other feline-related events when they seem more important to her than the humans, as on Thursday, 15 August 1940: 'I hear that one of the survivors of the torpedoed Transylvania came on shore with a cat in his arms, purring contentedly. Good!'[5] And on Tuesday, 29 October 1940: 'Went to call on a Paddington evacuee cat in the village, a sweet whitish kitten. The two dressmakers accompanying it are humbly grateful for their one room, where they can just squeeze in.'[6] But some cats don't have it easy. On a visit in early December 1940 to Southampton, which is badly bombed, Connie notes: '… a sad sight. Many forsaken cats sitting on the rubble.'[7]

It's illegal to give food which is suitable for human consumption to animals, including milk, though we know that Winston Churchill continues to feed his beloved ginger cat, Tango, with salmon from his own plate. But Lord Woolton, the Minister of Food, must also have a soft spot for cats when he announces at the New Year in 1942 that 'limited quantities of damaged dried milk … can be issued to owners of warehouses and other food stores in which cats are kept.' Apparently, some cats – even 'extraordinarily fussy' ones – love powdered milk while others hate it.[8] This bonus is only intended for 'working' cats who keep down the mice and rats but I'm sure no one would object to others receiving the milk too, such as the tabby who indicates to her profoundly deaf owner when the air-raid siren sounds. That cat could be a life-safer.

There are some touching stories about pets helping other pets. An inspector from the RSPCA rescues a scared and bedraggled tabby cat from a bombed-out building but, at the first opportunity, the cat goes back into the rubble. Further investigation discovers the cat beside a badly injured little dog. Only after the dog is rescued does the cat leave too.[9]

After that initial devastating destruction of pets, the government realises that they are good for morale and could be useful in the war effort. So, in a significant about turn, 'gas kennels' are manufactured for dogs, cats and small animals in case of gas attacks but these can cost up to £4 and, as the RSPCA points out, if anything happens to the owners, the animals might be forgotten and left to starve.[10] There is also advice on how to gas-proof bird cages.

An anti-gas kennel for a dog or other pet. IWM, GRM

Did You Know?

The RSPCA, which cares for animals in trouble, reported that thousands of school pets had to be taken into their care when children were evacuated and the schools abandoned. There were dogs, cats, rabbits, guineapigs and birds to be looked after and, at one London school, three baby alligators had to be dealt with![12]

Some animals even join the armed forces: Venus the bulldog is one particularly charismatic canine war hero in the Royal Navy. At a pet cemetery at Ilford in Essex, there is a headstone inscribed 'Here lies the noble Able Seacat, Simon', commemorating another Royal Navy mascot with the rank of Able Seaman.[11]

Surprisingly, although the famous Battersea Dogs Home in London has only four members of staff, they manage to care for 145,000 dogs during the war. Also, taking make do and mend to extremes, members are encouraged by the WI to collect fur from their dogs so it can be spun into knitting wool. Apparently, the hair from collies, sheepdogs, chows and Pekinese is best; Labradors', spaniels' and poodles' hair proves 'disappointing' and, overall, dog hair is inferior to sheep's wool.

Strange ideas to cope with the blackout

To travel safely is difficult without streetlights and with headlights, traffic lights and torches at a minimum in the blackout. Road traffic accidents increase alarmingly. Even in daylight, with signposts, milestones, railway station names and bus conductors no longer calling out the next stop – all to avoid aiding the enemy, if they should land here – it's all too easy to get confused while travelling, especially if the usual landmarks are now reduced to rubble. Without roadside signposts, Connie Miles wrote in her diary on Sunday,

24 November 1940: 'England is full of people gaily motoring up the wrong turning.'[13]

In the three months between the declaration of war in September 1930 and Christmas, over 4,000 pedestrians are killed in accidents during the blackout, whereas as there are only three fatalities during that period among the armed forces sent abroad. Something has to be done. Thick white lines are painted along the kerbs and around streetlights to make them more visible but this doesn't make much difference to road casualty numbers.

The government encourages people to 'Wear white at night', so they can be seen more clearly by drivers in the blackout but there are some innovative new products created to help, though the prices probably deterred all but the more affluent.

Selfridges store in London's Oxford Street introduces a range of luminous accessories. From 1940, they are selling silk flowers which glow in the dark to be worn by men as buttonholes on the lapel or by women as a corsage or hat decoration. Luminous badges and buttons for coats are made, costing a few pennies, and even doggy hi-vis jackets for walking your pet in the blackout. Luminous sticky tape to edge garments, armbands and walking sticks painted with luminous paint are other ideas. But, unfortunately, all these things are, in fact, radioactive![14] However, nobody worries about that or even understands the dangers at the time. But you'll know better and advise your friends against such biohazard fashions.

Less hazardous options are white raincoats or broad white collars to attach to your coat. Walking sticks with a torch at the tip to light your way or wave to hail a taxi are another innovation but they cost 14s 6d, as opposed to just 2s 6d for a luminous painted one. In order to hail a taxi or flag down a bus, a cheap option is to knit yourself a special pair of gloves: dark on the back of your hand but white on the palm so the driver can see it but the enemy flying overhead cannot. It is even forbidden to light a cigarette outside after blackout in case the match or lighter and the cigarette's orange glow are visible from above.

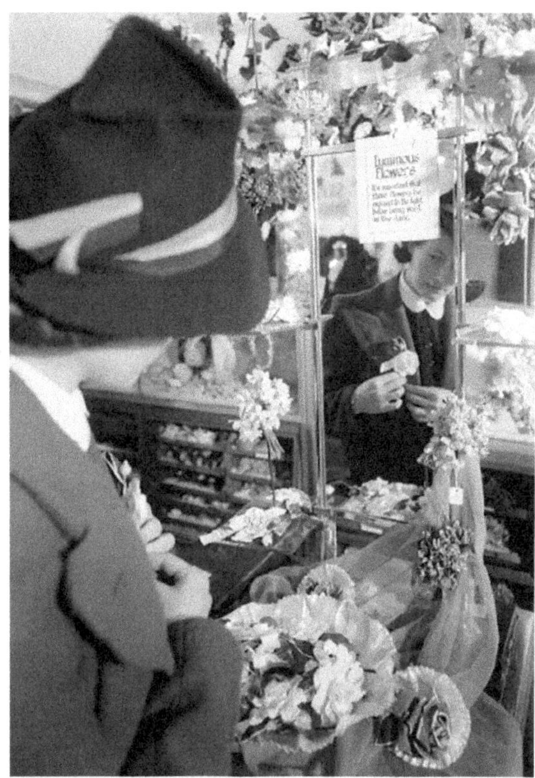

Right and below: Luminous flowers and doggy hi-vis jacket for sale in Selfridges. www.butterflybalcony.com/2013/10/the-home-front-blackout-accessories.html

The strange things people do

For those who want to remind themselves of the war effort – as if they could forget it! – patriotic textiles are available to make into dresses and blouses with motifs of aeroplanes or union flags.

The famous silk scarf manufacturer, Jacquard, prints scarves to remind people of war restrictions with slogans such as 'Watch what you say', 'Is your journey necessary?', 'Save and recycle' and many others.

Regarding fashion, one horrible idea suggested at the outset of war was that the whole population should wear a uniform to show we

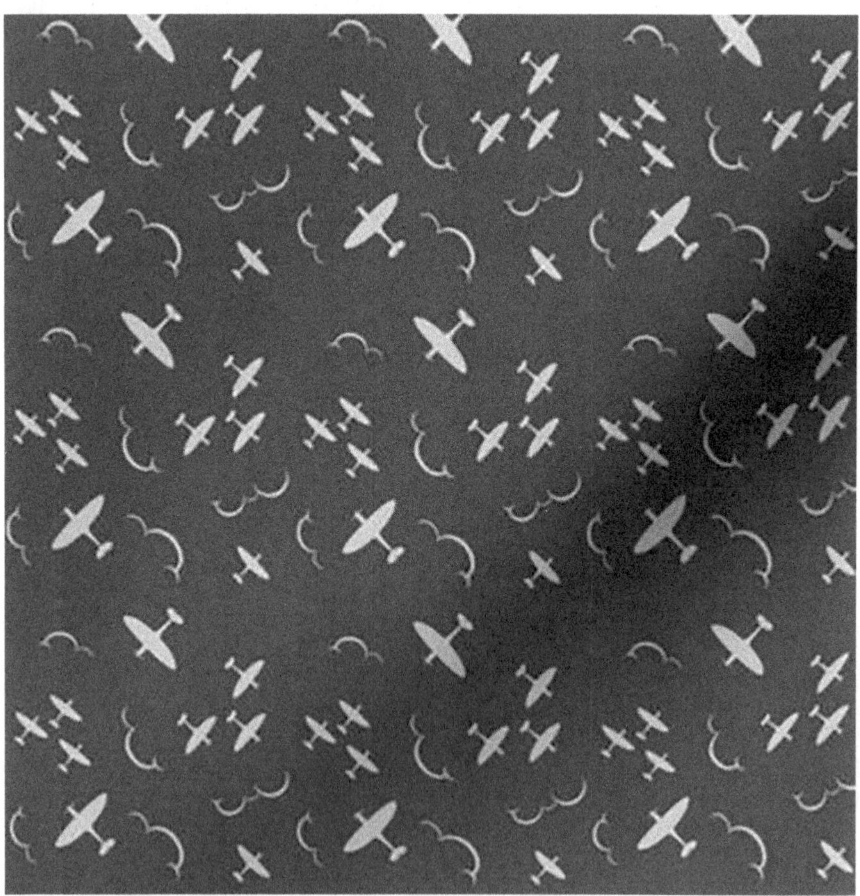

A reproduction patriotic printed Spitfire textile design. ELOISE_VARIN

Did You Know?

The Wrens' naval uniform is so stylish – in navy blue with a white shirt and the skirt slightly flared rather than tapered like those of other services, to make it easier to step on or off boats – after the war, the British Overseas Airways Corporation (BOAC) buys up surplus WRNS uniforms, including the tricorn officers' hats, for their air stewardesses' uniforms.

were united by the war effort. Fortunately, the idea was dismissed as being very bad for morale and probably impossible anyway.[15]

It's hard to believe, what with so many foods rationed or in short supply and all that downright hard work, the government is actually concerned that the population might get fat. With public swimming baths closed because fuel can't be wasted warming up the water and sea bathing off limits, someone comes up with the strange idea of dry swimming. To do this, put a chair without arms or a high stool in the middle of the room, well away from other furniture or anything breakable. Lie with your tummy across the chair and kick your feet and practise swimming strokes with your arms. For extra authenticity, put a second stool or chair under your face with a bowl of water to practise your swimming breathing at the same time. This is supposed to be good exercise… or maybe a not. A walk is probably better and far less bother.

But there are certainly those who spare no effort. One house-proud lady insists on dusting thoroughly before going to the shelter in case her home is bombed. If everyone can see inside, she doesn't want them to think the place isn't clean and spotless – the mess the bomb makes notwithstanding.[16]

During the 1940s, many women have their hair permanent waved or 'permed', if it doesn't curl naturally. Perming requires a lengthy visit to the hairdresser. A client's hair is washed, then comes the time-consuming application, strand by strand, of a potent chemical perming lotion before each strand is tightly wound around a curler. When all the hair is in curlers, the client has to sit under a heated hood hairdryer for up to an hour, until the 'perm' has 'taken'. Then the chemicals are washed out and neutralised, the hair put in plump rollers, dried again and finally styled. As you can imagine, there may be a problem: 'What if the air-raid siren goes while I'm under the hairdryer having my hair permed?' Fortunately, somebody has invented the Jamal method or 'freedom wave' which doesn't require sitting under a dryer but I don't know if it is very successful because it seems never to catch on.[17]

It may be even more risky to take a bath. During the night bombing, an ARP Warden, Harold Harthall of Morden in Surrey, hurries to a block of flats which has been badly damaged and rushes up the concrete stairs. In one flat, he discovers a woman who was taking a bath. The cast-iron bath has shattered in the blast, cutting her badly, and she is in shock. Harold carries her out and takes her to his own home nearby where he and his wife, Pat, give her a warm bath and pick out the metal shards from her body. They keep her warm until the ambulance arrives. In fact, the bather and Pat and a friend, Elsie, were fortunate. If they had made it to the air-raid shelter as intended, they may not have survived because the same bomb had destroyed it, killing ten people and seriously injuring others. Harold jokes that the woman he'd rescued from her bath always looks away whenever they pass in the street.[18]

There are changes in the way food products are presented and advertised which some people find strange, such as adverts which honestly admit you can't get their product any more but 'there'll be plenty after the war', such as that for Harlequin Sponge Puddings in *Picture Post* magazine, dated 26 February 1944. Robertson's Golden Shred marmalade states 'It will return with victory', and Idris, makers of lemon squash, apologise: 'Sorry… until peace returns there will be no more quality soft drink.' Other product advertising extols the wonderful wives who do two jobs, running the home while doing full-time war work as well. This opens up the possibility of a whole new range of food products aimed at making the housewife's struggle easier and less time consuming.

Invented in the US, packets of ready-weighed and mixed dry ingredients give her a short cut to cake and pudding making – just add an egg or milk – and these certainly catch on here in Britain and never look back. Breakfast cereal, also from the US, begins to partially replace the traditional 'full English' of sausage, egg, bacon, fried bread and all the trimmings. Most of the ingredients required are rationed and with time and fuel-saving at a premium, opening a packet of cornflakes is quick and easy. Mind you, this isn't considered to be a 'proper' breakfast.

To cheer up a bored cook – or make her life more difficult, depending on your point of view – the *Olio Cookery Book* comes up with this recipe for 'Bible Cake'. If you want to try it, you'll need a copy of The King James Bible as you have to look up the references to discover the ingredients needed but I've helped you out.

1. ½ lb Judges, ch.V, verse 25, last clause [butter]
2. ½ lb Jeremiah, ch.VI, verse 20 [sugar]
3. 1 tablespoon of I Samuel, ch.XIV, verse 25 [honey]
4. 3 of Jeremiah, ch.XVII, verse 11 [eggs]
5. ½ lb I Samuel, ch.XXX, verse 12 [raisins]
6. ½ lb Nahum, ch.III, verse 12 (chopped) [figs]
7. 2 oz Numbers, ch.XVII, verse 8 (blanched and chopped) [almonds]
8. 1 lb I Kings, ch.IV, verse 22 [flour]
9. Season to taste with II Chronicles, ch.IX, verse 9 [spices]
10. A pinch of Leviticus, ch.II, verse 13 [salt]
11. 1 teaspoon of Amos, ch.IV, verse 5 [leaven = baking powder]
12. 3 tablespoons Judges, ch. IV, verse 19 [water or milk]

Beat ingredients 1, 2 and 3 to a cream. Add 4, one at a time, still beating. Then add 5, 6 and 7 and beat again. In another bowl, mix together ingredients 8, 9, 10 and 11, and add to the creamed mixture a little at a time, then add 12. If necessary, add a little extra Exodus, ch.III, verse 17, third word from the end [milk], to moisten the mixture.

Bake in a slow oven [140–150°C, 275–300°F, Gas Mark 1–2 for 1½ hours. Enjoy your well-earned Bible Cake].

The ration book diet can be very tedious, especially for children who aren't keen on vegetables. Connie Miles has this to say in her diary on Thursday, 29 August 1940:

> Went to serve the evacuated children in the canteen. They all seemed very little and shabby and held their spoons in a firm grip. 'No cabbage!' cried so many of these tiny mites. I said severely to some little girls, 'You'll never grow up pretty … unless you eat cabbage.' One looked up and said, 'Shall I grow pretty if I eat cabbage?' 'Yes, indeed,' I said. 'Then I don't want to be pretty,' she replied firmly.[19]

But there are worse things than cabbage. One afternoon at the end of the war, 13-year-old Jane Brown of Heaton, Newcastle-upon-Tyne, smells something cooking. In the kitchen, a big pot is simmering on the stove. She lifts the lid and sees… a horror: a whole sheep's head, complete with eyeballs and long, brown teeth, is boiling in the pot. Apparently, it was the only thing Mrs Brown had enough coupons for by the time she reached the front of the queue at the butcher's.[20]

Deceiving the enemy

A ploy to deceive the enemy is hatched after the Super Marine Spitfire factories in Southampton are destroyed on 26 September 1940. Aeroplane construction is moved out across southern England, to Reading, Hungerford and other towns in secret locations. In Salisbury in particular, the local Wiltshire & Dorset Bus Co. Garage, the Sunlight Laundry, A. J. Waters Garage and the Wessex Motor Works are among the buildings turned to Spitfire production while looking otherwise unchanged.[21]

A young hairdresser, Bette Blackwell, becomes a riveter at the Wessex Motor Works, where she works from 8.00 am–8.00 pm or

8.00 pm–8.00 am, on a monthly rota. She remembers that for ages they had no idea how the fuselages and wings they were making left the factory until one occasion when she saw the entire end wall, which looked so solid, folded up like a concertina so the parts could be taken on trailers to High Post a few miles away for final assembly.

Joan Johns works at Wellworthies Spitfire Factory, testing piston rings in the laboratory; Joan Borough progresses from washing out oil filters to fixing propellers. High Post also has an experimental department where Stella Rutter is a draughtswoman, designing and constantly improving aeroplane technology.

Chattis Hill is the secret factory and airfield about twelve miles from Salisbury where final test flights are conducted and new technology is tried out. When the hangars were built, as far as possible, trees were bent aside, rather than felled, so they could then be released to stand upright again and hide the buildings from the air. Completed Spitfires are hidden in back gardens and copses, awaiting the ATA girls to fly them out to the aerodromes. Joy Lofthouse learned to fly before she could drive and says that, although they are paid to ferry the planes, 'all they want to do is fly and fly' and would do the job for nothing.

Mary Wilkins-Ellis, another ATA pilot, agrees with one of the male test pilots that a Spitfire 'is a lady in the air but a bitch on the ground'. Apparently, while taxiing, the pilot cannot see where they're going because the nose of the aircraft is so high and blocks their view, so planes zig-zag along the runway until they're fast enough for the tail to begin to lift and tilts the nose down. On Mary's first time ever flying a Spitfire, a member of the ground crew asks her how many she has flown. He falls backwards in shock when she says, 'None.'

The little factories are so well disguised even the locals aren't aware of them and those who work there have to sign the Official Secrets Act, including the young telegraph boy, Gordon Topp, who delivers telegrams with new orders to the sites. Salisbury produces about 10 per cent of the 22,000 Spitfires flown during the war, of which 15,000 are lost to enemy action.

Britain lacks the brute force, manpower and equipment to defeat the mighty German war machine, even with US aid and thousands of GIs to bolster the numbers. Therefore, subtler methods have to be used. Before the D-Day landings in Normandy in Northern France in June 1944, a vast project, Operation Bodyguard,[22] is set up to deceive the enemy, to give the impression that the landings will be in Calais, much farther east. Calais is the closest point on the European mainland to Britain, just twenty miles across the English Channel from Dover in Kent.

Operation Bodyguard involves making Kent appear to be the focus of troop preparations with hundreds of planes, tanks, guns and vehicles being assembled. To German pilots, seeing this from the air, so much equipment can mean only one thing: the invasion force will land in Calais and the Germans move their armies and build massive defences there to repel the combined British, US and Canadian forces. However, the planes are full-size inflatable dummies, the tanks are cardboard, the guns are of printed canvas over a wooden framework and the vehicles are fake too. Professional magicians, skilled in sleight-of-hand and deceiving the eye, advise on the construction of these models to fool the enemy, as do theatre stage scenery experts.

Another aspect of Operation Bodyguard is giving false information to the enemy. MI5 – the British Secret Service – has a handful of German spies who, unknown to the enemy, are working for us. We know the identity of every German spy working here thanks to Bletchley Park decoding all the Enigma messages. Arrested and given the choice of being tried for treason – the punishment for which is hanging – they agree to be double agents, sending false information back to Berlin about the D-Day plans.

They're so successful, they not only convince the enemy that Calais is the target but that a second mighty force is assembling on the east coast of England and Scotland in preparation to invade German-occupied Norway. The purpose of this is to keep German forces in Norway and prevent them from reinforcing France. In fact, there is no east coast army at all except in the spies' messages to Berlin and we know Hitler believes all this fictitious information because the Enigma messages confirm it. Hitler even awards his supposedly most reliable spy in England the Iron Cross medal. This same man is later awarded the Member of the British Empire (MBE) medal by the king in thanks for his fantastic contribution to the British war effort.

Carrier pigeons are used occasionally to bring messages home from Europe and there are fears that German pigeons might 'infiltrate' this secret business. Basil Thomson, a Scotland Yard spy-catcher, recorded that 'It was positively dangerous to be seen in conversation with a pigeon. Some experts claimed to be able to identify a pigeon with a German "accent".'[23]

Seriously?

Nothing to do with deception and more about being lucky, during the London Blitz, all the bridges across the River Thames survive intact apart from the loss of a decorative parapet here and an ornamental finial there. This is incredible because the enemy bombers use the river as a guide to their targets. How can they possibly miss targeting every bridge?[24]

In broadcasting on the wireless, Wilfred Pickles is employed by the BBC because of his broad northern accent – this when listeners expected 'proper' pronunciation or, as one person put it: 'radio announcers should sound as though they are wearing evening dress' – which, in fact, they do for evening programmes, even though listeners can't see them. The idea of using Wilfred's regional voice is that it will be far more difficult for German infiltrators to impersonate but,

Did You Know?

Apparently, female voices carry better than male over radio transmissions and the noise of aircraft cockpits, so German-speaking girls are trained to imitate their counterparts in the Luftwaffe's fighter control, issuing contradictory instructions over the radio and confusing the enemy pilots, saving Allied lives.

at first, listeners are 'shocked' by the way Wilfred speaks, although he becomes quite a radio personality, eventually, once listeners get used to his accent.

Recycling – more strange stories

Everyone is encouraged to recycle everything they possibly can and metal is the most obvious precious commodity, with many innovative methods being tried to reclaim it. Many trophies from the Great War of 1914–1918, such as German field guns or presentation tanks that survived, are collected for salvage. In the Paddington area of London, there is a campaign branded as 'A Mile of Keys', the collection of a million unused keys, though we don't know whether the target is reached or not.[25]

But what happens to all this metal is the subject of various rumours, including these: that Bomber Command drops it on Germany, or the metal is being used for ballast in ships or, as one story goes, the 'seaport buildings in Nigeria sport rather nice Georgian railings'.

A later popular theory originates in 1984, when a letter to the *Evening Standard* newspaper claims that, according to dockers in Canning Town, 'many hundreds of tons of scrap iron and ornamental railings were sent to the bottom of the Thames Estuary'. During the war, the men had worked on lighters that were towed down the Thames to dump surplus quantities of scrap metal and decorative ironwork. They claim that so much was deposited at certain spots, such as off Sheerness, that passing ships' compasses were affected by the quantity of iron resting on the seabed. Similar dumping is said to have occurred in the Solent, between Southampton and the Isle of Wight and in the Irish Sea, but there has never been any official confirmation – nor, conversely, any explanation as to how hundreds of thousands of tons of old iron suddenly disappeared.

Another odd event which occurred after the war happened in 1968. Ex-ATA Hurricane pilot, Joan Hughes, was prosecuted for dangerous flying after she flew a Tiger Moth under a motorway bridge. She was actually playing the 'stunt double' for Lady Penelope, a puppet character in the film *Thunderbird 6*, at the time and was acquitted on all charges.[26]

Double British Summer Time

As you're a time-traveller, it may interest you to know that, during the war, we have something called Double British Summer Time. DBST adds two hours to Greenwich Mean Time, which is the true time according to the sun when it is overhead at midday. On DBST the sun is overhead at 2.00pm by the clock. The explanation is that in midsummer in southern England, the sun rises at 4.00am GMT and 5.00am according to British Summer Time as used in peace time when we put the clocks forward by an hour at the end of March.

Nobody wants to begin the working day so early but during the war this is reckoned to be 'a waste of precious daylight'. To 'increase productivity for the war effort', the government decides that DBST is the answer. People will be getting up at 4.00am, according to the sun and GMT, but the clock will tell them it's 6.00am. This is brilliant in the summer but not so good in winter when we only have seven or so hours of daylight and normally return to GMT at the end of October. In the war, we don't revert to GMT but use the plus one hour BST throughout the winter. Unfortunately, this means horrible dark mornings while travelling to work or school but it doesn't get dark quite so early for the journey home as it does when we revert to GMT in October 1945.

On which note, let's now turn our attention to what things will be like after the war ends and peace returns. When will our lives return to normal?

Chapter 10

When Will It End?

No doubt, everyone celebrating Victory in Europe Day (VE Day) on Tuesday, 8 May 1945 and Victory over Japan Day (VJ Day) on Wednesday, 15 August 1945 hopes that things are about to get better. But the truth is that they become worse. Rationing continues for another nine years after the war ends and austerity increases. For the eight months from 1 September 1945 until 30 April 1946, coupons are reduced to just twenty-four per person – only three coupons a month. Food rationing, which began as a wartime measure in January 1940, is extended into peace time because Britain's economy is in ruins.

We may have defeated the enemy but the country is virtually bankrupt, having lost nearly 30 per cent of the nation's wealth, and British exports are reduced to almost nothing. To make matters more dire, in August 1945, the US ends its Lend-Lease programme, plunging the newly elected Labour government into crisis. We now depend on loans from the US and Canada to keep our economy afloat and everyone endures years of financial hardship. Bread and potatoes – never rationed during the war – are now added to the list of rationed food in 1946 and 1947 respectively.

Did You Know?

Yes, it seems crazy but, in June 1946, cricket balls go on the ration due to a shortage of cork which forms the main central core of the ball.

As Elizabeth Bowen describes the wartime High Street in town, it's a sorry-looking place:

> The main street was by now empty: today nothing more would happen. Before noon the housewives had swarmed … stripping the shops so that one might ask why these remained open. A scale or two adhered to the fishmonger's marble slab; the pastry-cook's glass shelves showed a range of interesting crumbs; the fruiterer filled a long-standing void with fans of cardboard bananas and a 'Dig for Victory' placard; the greengrocer's crates had been emptied of all but earth by those who had somehow failed to dig hard enough. The butcher flaunted unknown joints of purplish meat in the confidence that these could not be bought; the dairy restricted itself to a china cow; the grocer, with costless courage, kept intact his stocks of dummy cartons and tins. In the confectioner's windows the ribbons bleach on dummy boxes of chocolates among fly-blown cut-outs of pre-war blondes. Newsagents without newspapers gave out in angry red chalk that they had no matches either. Pasted inside the telephone booth, a notice asked one to telephone less.[1]

But it isn't bad news for everyone. Children have a different perspective on life after the war. Let's ask Richard Mann about his childhood in Camberwell Gate, Walworth, in East London:

'Hello, Richard. Would you like to tell us how you and your friends have fun these days?'

'Oh, we have the best playgrounds ever. We go in the bombed-out ruins, down in the basements, upstairs and through doors that don't lead nowhere anymore. And we have our dads', grandfathers' and uncles' cast-offs from the war, you know, their tin helmets, webbing off their old uniforms and gas masks and stuff like that, so we play at battles and even Blackie the dog wears a helmet. Don't know who he belongs to but he likes to join in.'

'Where's your favourite place to play?'

'East Street, where St Mark's is, though we don't go in there 'cos it's a church, in the bombed-out houses on Lytham Street, Arnside Street and Albany Road. Best of all, we like going to the old air-raid shelter tunnels by the Elephant and Castle [a famous old pub]. It's pitch dark in them but we're brave, mostly, except one time when we disturbed an old drunk down there and he scared us. We never ran so fast…'

'Do you ever get into trouble?'

'Nah, not really, but I scrape my knees a lot and then Mum puts a horrible hot white poultice – she says it's kaolin – on them grazes but it's not that bad. One time, me and my mates got something called impetigo. They said we caught it from playing in the builders' sand what the cats and dogs use as a toilet. You should've seen us! We was all painted with this purple stuff [gentian violet] and looked like we had mauve chickenpox.'

'What happens in the winter? Do you still play outside in the cold weather?'

'Yeah, o' course we do. We're used to getting chapped legs, what with always wearing short trousers. Mum puts Vaseline on them which sticks your knees together. We go out and collect up the old tarry blocks…'

'What are they? I've never heard of tarry blocks.'

'You haven't? Well, see, the old tram lines, what the council is ripping up these days, were set in these blocks of wood which is covered in tar paper. The council leaves piles of them by the road and nobody wants them. They burn ever so well and Mum puts them on the fire to make our bit of coal go further. Trouble is they make thick black smoke and set us all coughing. Mum took me to the doctor 'cos of the cough and I got given extra orange juice – nice – and cod liver oil – yuk! And extra milk at school.'

'Is that the worst thing?'

'Nah. Worse than that is when Mum gives me thruppence [3d] and tells me to go and buy a bundle of firewood from Woodall's the greengrocer. Every week it happens and I know what's coming next... Mum and Nan heat up a load of water on the fire and then they fetch the tin bath... I hate having a bath with that horrible soap. I don't know why I have to when I just go out and get dirty again. Seems like a waste of time... a waste of thruppence too.'

'I'm sure your mother doesn't think so but thank you for talking to us, Richard.'[2]

Things can only get better

Life remains difficult after the war but, by the end of the 1940s, Britain's financial position is gradually improving, partly because of the generous US Marshall Aid, also the Labour government's efficient management of the economy and the devaluation of the pound in 1949 which makes British goods cheaper to foreign buyers, bringing back lost customers and making our exports more popular.

Making life better for everyone, in 1947, the government creates the National Health Service (NHS), providing free health care for everyone – an incredible advance in social welfare for all. Slowly, rationing is coming to an end: bread in July 1948; jam, treacle and syrup in December 1948; clothes rationing is abolished in 1949; petrol in 1950; tea on 3 October 1952. Sweets come off in February 1953; eggs in March that year; cream in April and sugar in September. Butter, margarine, cooking fats and cheese come off the ration in May 1954 and, finally, on 4 July that year, meat and bacon rationing ends – a day of rejoicing for everyone but vegetarians!

In the Heaton area of Newcastle-upon-Tyne, before sweet rationing ends, young Jane Brown, who was 6 years old when the war began, is happy to sell her sweet coupons to her elder sister, Margery, in order

A 1947 advertisement for Tattoo lipstick

to buy sewing materials. The plan is that Margery will get fat and Jane will have nicer clothes to wear. A double result for Jane![3]

With the return of their products to the shops, manufacturers go crazy with their advertising campaigns, like the one shown from 1947 for Tattoo lipstick.

The illustration shows a naked woman in a jungle setting, back view only, with flowers in her hair and impossibly red pouting lips:

> Yes! It's Tattoo's secret... this lip magic... this South Seas difference! Yes... no other lipstick is like it... provocative... ultra-vivid... glamour-laden. And lastingly, reassuringly, serenely unmoved by time, teacups cocktails and kisses.
>
> It's Tattoo's South Secret... stain for lips instead of greasy coating! Never smearing... no matter what! Dawn-dewy... dainty! You put it on... let it set... wipe it off... and only the lasting colour remains.
>
> Daring shades... enchanting as lagoon-side flowers... NATURAL, TAHITI ROSE, TROPIC DAWN... for the kiss of the sun... EXOTIC, HAWAIIAN, CORAL... and for romance that steals in the dusk... PAGAN RED, BLACK MAGIC, ORCHID.
>
> Soul-stirring shades that thrill men's hearts...

It sounds more like a bodice-ripper novel than a lipstick advert, with all those 'dot, dot, dots' doesn't it?

And every woman wants a new wardrobe. At first, surplus forces' uniforms are put to good use by skilled dressmakers. Naval 'whites', the hot-climate uniforms, make excellent summer skirts and tennis dresses. Scottish regimental tartans are snapped up and remade into winter skirts and casual trousers. But, at last, fashion returns.

In 1947, Christian Dior, one of the leading Paris fashion houses, introduces their 'New Look' designs. Every newspaper and magazine carries pictures of this latest fashion with nipped-in waists, soft

Marks & Spencer's 'New Look' advertisement

shoulder lines and billowing skirts. These feminine, flowing designs are in complete contrast to the square shoulders and straight skirts of uniforms and Utility clothing – though this scheme continues until 1952. It's such a refreshing change and you, like so many other women, probably want at least one 'New Look' outfit in your meagre wardrobe, but who can afford Parisian *haute couture* prices? Fortunately, High Street stores soon produce their own ranges and paper patterns quickly become available for those who can sew, though textiles may still require coupons and be in short supply.

You may think that all you need is the pattern, the cloth and a sewing machine and a new dress is yours in no time. But think again. It may not be so straightforward, as this advice from the *Singer Sewing Machine Manual* of 1949 makes clear:

> Prepare yourself mentally for sewing. Think about what you are going to do. Never approach sewing with a sigh or lackadaisically. Good results are difficult when indifference dominates. Never try to sew with a sink full of dirty dishes or beds unmade.
>
> When there are urgent housekeeping chores, do these first so that your mind is free to enjoy your sewing. When you sew, make yourself as attractive as possible. Put on a clean dress. Keep a little bag of French chalk near your sewing machine to dust your fingers at intervals. Have your hair in order, powder and lipstick put on. If you are constantly fearful that a visitor might drop in or your husband will come home, and you will not look neatly put together, you will not enjoy your sewing.

Hey! I'm making a dress; not having an affair with the machine. Can you believe this nonsense? The sad fact is that now the war effort has ended, all the women who were in the services, or working in factories, doing men's jobs or simply found themselves as head-of-household are now expected to meekly go back to the kitchen sink and do so quietly without a word of protest.

Getting back to normal

'Normal' in this man's world means that a woman's 'proper' place is as a wife, homemaker and carer, subservient to men as before the war. It's now made plain that they were only 'temporarily drafted in' to do men's work during the emergency and now demobbed men expect to have their jobs back and a wife to return home to in the evening with a cooked meal ready for them. Some women are probably glad, relieved to have things back as they were in 1939. But for others who have tasted independence, earning their own income, often with considerable responsibilities outside the home, the old ways are not so welcome.

Teenage girls at the start of the war have watched their mothers take over the workforce and, later, joined up themselves or worked the land or made munitions. Now they are expected to give up work, get married and quietly raise the next generation. The men want them looking pretty and doing as they're told. But I think even they must realise not all girls want this.

Things have changed. But men hope to put the clock back and the school system does its best to re-educate girls with lessons such as this on *How to be a Good Wife*, from a home economics textbook of 1954:

> When your husband returns home from work –
>
> - Have his dinner ready. Plan ahead: this will let him know you have been thinking of him.
> - Prepare yourself. Take 15 minutes to rest, touch up your make-up, put a ribbon in your hair.
> - Be a little gay. His boring day will need a lift.
> - Clear away the clutter. Collect up the children toys and dust the tables: your husband will feel he has reached a haven of rest and order.
> - Prepare the children. Brush their hair: they are his little treasures and he would like to see them play their part.
> - Encourage the children to be quiet and happy to see him.

- Greet him with a warm smile and be pleased he is home.
- DON'T greet him with problems or complain if he is late.
- Make him comfortable. Suggest he lies down and prepare a drink for him.
- Arrange his pillow and take off his shoes.
- Speak in a soothing pleasant voice.
- Listen to him. You may have so much to tell him but let him speak first.
- Make the evening his. DON'T complain if he doesn't take you out to dinner.
- Try to understand his world of strain and pressure.
- DON'T question his decisions or his actions. He is master of the house and you have no right to question him.
- A GOOD WIFE ALWAYS KNOWS HER PLACE.

Wow! Are you spitting mad or laughing until your ribs hurt? It's hard to believe this was written in a school textbook, isn't it? The wife sounds more like a poor, lowly, Victorian serving maid. No wonder this generation of schoolgirls went on to burn their bras!

School girls who had lessons like this! www.wiganworld.co.uk

Conclusion

Rationing ended completely in July 1954 and became just one aspect of the war which had been fought as vigorously on the Home Front as it had in foreign fields, in the air and at sea. Life was hard and austere but we came through. Victory was celebrated in 1945 but the fight continued at home for another nine years until Britain finally achieved its economic victory. This period of our history saw bleak, dark days of hardship illuminated by sparks of humour and the occasional lights of heroism.

I hope you have enjoyed this adventure back to the 1940s and early 1950s to experience life when Britain was 'on the ration'. If this little collection of stories, information and tips helps you to survive in Ration Book Britain, though your time-travelling takes you no farther than your sofa, my efforts will have been worthwhile.

Notes

Chapter 1: Introduction

1. S. V. Partington (editor), *Mrs Miles's Diary: The Wartime Journal of a Housewife on the Home Front* (Simon & Schuster, 2013), pp. 227–228.
2. Ibid., pp. 321–322.

Chapter 2: Where Would I Live?

1. Text taken and adapted from two British Electrical Development Association advertisements, c. 1939.
2. My thanks go to Christine and Jeff Sherman for this snippet of family history concerning Jeff's parents.
3. My thanks go to Linda Gorman, a volunteer at the Old Forge World War II House, 26 East Street, Sittingbourne, Kent, for this story of her evacuation.
4. There were 1,500,000 children evacuated according to government figures but 3,000,000, according to the National Archives.
5. S. V. Partington (editor), *Mrs Miles's Diary: The Wartime Journal of a Housewife on the Home Front* (Simon & Schuster, 2013), p. 200.
6. Mike Brown, *Evacuees of the Second World War* (Shire Publications Ltd., 2009), pp. 25–27.
7. At the time, asbestos was considered a marvellous material, being an excellent insulator which is fire-proof. Nobody realised then that asbestos is carcinogenic if its fluffy fibres are inhaled.

Chapter 3: What Would I Eat?

1. Published by Cambridge University Press (first edition 1940; this second edition 1942).
2. My thanks go to Christine Beech of the Gravesend Writing Group for this family tale told to the author.
3. Edna Healey, *The Queen's House: A Social History of Buckingham Palace* (Pegasus Books, 2012), p. 275.
4. Twigs Way and Mike Brown, *Digging for Victory* (Sabrestorm Publishing, 2010), p. 167.
5. My thanks go to Marion Cashman for her memories as told to the author.
6. Amy Thomas was my maternal grandmother and this interview is based on her reminiscences. Her younger son was killed on his first sea voyage with the Royal Navy.
7. www.bbc.co.uk/food/recipes/woolton_pie_98706
8. Mike Brown, *Evacuees of the Second World War* (Shire Publications, 2009), p. 38–39.
9. Marguerite Patten OBE, *Victory Cookbook, 1940–54* (Imperial War Museum, 2005), no page numbers.
10. Susie Hodge, *The Home Front in World War Two* (Pen & Sword, 2012), p. 51.
11. S. V. Partington (editor), *Mrs Miles's Diary* (Simon & Schuster, 2013), p. 296.

Chapter 4: How Can I Keep Healthy and Safe?

1. 'The Hedgerow Harvest', Ministry of Food (1943 or 1945).
2. https://frostysramblings.wordpress.com/2017/12/29/wild-plants-that-won-the-wars
3. My thanks to Paul Bayliss for this latter information.
4. Tessa Dunlop, *The Bletchley Girls* (Hodder & Stoughton, 2015), p. 59.

5. Freely adapted from a number of sources, including Susie Hodge, *The Home Front in World War Two* (Pen & Sword, 2012), pp. 5–24.
6. Susie Hodge, *The Home Front in World War Two* (Pen & Sword, 2012), pp. 17–18.

Chapter 5: What Jobs Could I Do?

1. Tessa Dunlop, *The Bletchley Girls* (Hodder & Stoughton, 2015), p. 84.
2. S. V. Partington (editor), *Mrs Miles's Diary* (Simon & Schuster, 2013), p. 317.
3. Freely adapted from Giles Whittell, *Spitfire Women of World War II* (Harper Perennial, 2008) with reference to Diana Barnato.
4. Ruth Mansergh, *Wimbledon, Merton & Morden at War 1939–45* (Pen & Sword Military, 2018), p. 140.
5. S. V. Partington (editor), *Mrs Miles's Diary* (Simon & Schuster, 2013), pp. 300–302.
6. Footnote in S. V. Partington (editor), *Mrs Miles's Diary* (Simon & Schuster, 2013).
7. https://en.wikipedia.org/wiki/The_Thing-Ummy_Bob
8. Tessa Dunlop, *The Bletchley Girls* (Hodder & Stoughton, 2015), pp. 125–126.

Chapter 6: What Would I Wear?

1. Julia Summers, *Fashion on the Ration* (Profile Books, 2016), p. 10.
2. Ibid., p. 6.
3. Ibid., p. 12.
4. My thanks go to Marion Cashman for her memories as told to the author.

5. Julia Summers, *Fashion on the Ration* (Profile Books, 2016), p. 132.
6. www.tuppencehapenny.com/blog/put-your-best-face-forward-yardley-1942-43

Chapter 7: How Could I Keep Calm and Carry On?

1. www.nuffieldfoundation.org/sites/default/files/files/Lord%20Nuffield%20Philanthropic%20Legacy.pdf
2. Tessa Dunlop, *The Bletchley Girls* (Hodder & Stoughton, 2015), pp. 55–56.
3. Mike Brown and Carol Harris, *The Wartime House* (Sutton Publishing, 2005), p. 154.
4. S. V. Partington (editor), *Mrs Miles's Diary* (Simon & Schuster, 2013), p. 235.
5. Ibid., p. 163.
6. Ibid., p. 193.
7. Ibid., p. 243.
8. Mike Brown, *Christmas on the Home Front* (Sutton Publishing, 2004), p. 14.
9. Written from what Mum told me long ago. My parents did have quite a happy life with three children – including me – though we were slow to come along. Sadly, Joyce died in 1972 but Lofty – ever a man of few words – was with us until 2002. After their wedding, he was posted to patrolling the North Atlantic as a wireless operator on an Icelandic trawler, *Elvig*, which was, in fact, a spy vessel and as Dad wasn't in naval uniform for this but dressed as a fisherman, if captured, he could've been shot as a spy.
10. My thanks go to Wendy Ahl for this information.
11. S. V. Partington (editor), *Mrs Miles's Diary* (Simon & Schuster, 2013), p. 226.
12. Ibid., p. 203.

Chapter 8: How Could I Do My Bit to Support the War Effort?

1. www.keymilitary.com/article/waste-helped-win-war
2. Ibid.
3. Records suggest only 26 per cent of the ironwork collected was used for munitions and, by 1945, much of it was quietly rusting in depots or in overgrown village dumps.
4. http://vandwdestroyerassociation.org.uk/Warship_Weeks.html
5. S. V. Partington (editor), *Mrs Miles's Diary* (Simon & Schuster, 2013), p. 299.
6. Mike Brown and Carol Harris, *The Wartime House* (Sutton Publishing, 2005), p. 166–167.
7. Freely adapted from Julia Summers, *Fashion on the Ration* (Profile Books, 2016), pp. 47–51.
8. Something Royal Mail, with its bar-coded stamps, post-coded letters and no bombs falling, constantly fails to do in the twenty-first century despite a first-class stamp, 'guaranteeing' next-day delivery, costing £1.65 for a standard-sized letter (current in January 2025).
9. www.postalmuseum.org/blog/the-post-office-during-wwii

Chapter 9: Strange But True

1. Clare Campbell, *Bonzo's War: Animals Under Fire, 1939–45* (Constable, 2013), p. 148.
2. www.iwm.org.uk/history/9-famous-animals-from-the-first-and-second-world-wars
3. S. V. Partington (editor), *Mrs Miles's Diary* (Simon & Schuster, 2013), p. 140.
4. Ibid., p. 192.
5. Ibid., p. 150. The *Transylvania* had been sunk on 10 August off Malin Head, Ireland.

6. Ibid., p. 176.
7. Ibid., p. 187.
8. Clare Campbell, *Bonzo's War: Animals Under Fire, 1939–45* (Constable, 2013), pp. 236–237.
9. Ibid., pp. 158–159.
10. Mike Brown and Carol Harris, *Air Raids & Ration Books* (Sabrestorm Publishing, 2010), pp. 18–19.
11. www.atlasobscura.com/articles/british-pet-massacre
12. Mike Brown, *Evacuees of the Second World War* (Shire Publications Ltd., 2009), p. 33.
13. S. V. Partington (editor), *Mrs Miles's Diary* (Simon & Schuster, 2013), p. 180.
14. Mike Brown and Carol Harris, *Air Raids & Ration Books* (Sabrestorm Publishing, 2010), p. 24.
15. Julia Summers, *Fashion on the Ration* (Profile Books, 2016), p. 35.
16. My thanks go to Christine Cottrell for this story about her house-proud nan.
17. Mike Brown and Carol Harris, *Air Raids & Ration Books* (Sabrestorm Publishing, 2010), advertisement, p. 30.
18. My thanks go to Sue Jeeves of the Gravesend Writing Group for this story of her parents in Morden, Surrey.
19. S. V. Partington (editor), *Mrs Miles's Diary* (Simon & Schuster, 2013), pp. 155–156.
20. My thanks go to Kate Haines of the Rochester U3A Writing Group for this story of her mother's childhood in Newcastle.
21. *Secret Spitfires*, a Channel 4 programme first broadcast in 2017 and on 26 April 2024.
22. *Double Cross: The True Story of the D-day Spies*, presented by Ben MacIntyre, first broadcast on BBC2 on 9 July 2012 and on BBC FOUR on 29 May 2024.
23. Ben MacIntyre, *Double Cross: The True Story of the D-Day Spies* (Bloomsbury, 2016), p. 118.

24. S. V. Partington (editor), *Mrs Miles's Diary* (Simon & Schuster, 2013), p. 195.
25. Austin J. Ruddy, 31 December 2020 (online).
26. Giles Whittell, *Spitfire Women of World War II* (Harper Perennial, 2008), p. 279.

Chapter 10: When Will It End?

1. Elizabeth Bowen, *The Heat of the Day*, 1949, excerpt from the novel.
2. Freely adapted from Richard Mann, *Memories of a Walworth Childhood 1945–1965*, https://walworthsaintpeter.blogspot.com/2013/12/memories-of-walworth-childhood-1945-1965.html (posted Friday, 13 December 2013).
3. My thanks go to Kate Haines of the Rochester U3A Writing Group for this story of her mother's childhood in Newcastle.

Bibliography

Please note: there are so many brilliant books available dealing with various aspects of life in Ration Book Britain, but I have marked (*) those which I found most useful and/or a riveting read.

Brown, Mike, *Christmas on the Home Front* (Sutton Publishing, 2004)

Brown, Mike & Harris, Carol, *The Wartime House* (Sutton Publishing, 2005)

Brown, Mike, *Evacuees of the Second World War* (Shire Publications Ltd., 2009)

*Brown, Mike & Harris, Carol, *Air Raids & Ration Books* (Sabrestorm Publishing, 2010)

Brown, Mike, et al., *The Ration Book Diet* (The History Press, 2023)

Bourne, Dr Geoffrey, *Nutrition & The War* (Cambridge University Press, 1939)

*Campbell, Clare, *Bonzo's War: Animals Under Fire, 1939–45* (Constable, 2013)

Dixon, Barbara (compiler & editor), *Wartime Scrapbook* (Collins & Brown, 2005)

*Dunlop, Tessa, *The Bletchley Girls* (Hodder & Stoughton, 2015)

*Harris, Carol, *Women at War in Uniform* (Sutton Publishing, 2003)

*Hodge, Susie, *The Home Front in World War Two* (Pen & Sword, 2012)

Holyoake, Gregory, *The Prefab Kid* (S. B. Publications, 1998)

*MacIntyre, Ben, *Double Cross: The True Story of the D-day Spies* (Bloomsbury, 2016)

Mansergh, Ruth, *Wimbledon, Merton & Morden at War 1939–45* (Pen & Sword Military, 2018). Kindly lent by Sue Jeeves

Norman, Jill, *Make Do and Mend* (Michael O'Mara Books, 2007)

Orr, John Boyd, *Food, Health and Income* (MacMillan & Co. Ltd, London, 1937). With grateful thanks to Annie Tomkins

*Partington, S. V. (editor), *Mrs Miles's Diary* (Simon & Schuster, 2013)

Patten, Marguerite, OBE, *Victory Cookbook 1940–54* (Imperial War Museum, 2005)

*Starns, Penny and Legg, Penny, *Escaping the Blitz* (Sabrestorm Publishing, 2021). Kindly lent by Richard Miller

Storey, Neil R. and Housego, Molly, *Women in the Second World War* (Shire Publications, 2011)

*Summers, Julia, *Fashion on the Ration* (Profile Books, 2016)

Taylor, Eric, *Heroines of World War II* (Robert Hale, London, 1995)

Turner, Barry & Rennell, Tony, *When Daddy Came Home* (Pimlico, 1995)

Way, Twigs & Brown, Mike, *Digging for Victory* (Sabrestorm Publishing, 2010)

*Whittell, Giles, *Spitfire Women of World War II* (Harper Perennial, 2008)

Websites

Time Magazine: https://time.com/5764204/wwii-home-front-britain

Mass Observation Project: www.massobs.org.uk

Mass Observation Project on Evacuees: www.massobs.org.uk/images/booklets/Evacuation.pdf

BBC People's War: www.bbc.co.uk/history/ww2peopleswar/categories/c08

GI Handbook: https://flashbak.com/1942-extracts-from-gi-handbook-instructions-for-american-servicemen-in-britain-14231

Jobs for women: https://heritagecalling.com/2020/03/01/women-in-the-workforce-during-the-second-world-war-taking-on-mens-roles

The Post Office in World War II: www.postalmuseum.org/blog/the-post-office-during-wwii

Royal Army Pay Corps: https://rapc-association.org.uk/pay-services-history/ww2/during-ww2.html
Air Transport Auxiliary: www.kenleyrevival.org/content/history/women-at-war/air-transport-auxiliary
Clothes rationing: www.iwm.org.uk/history/8-facts-about-clothes-rationing-in-britain-during-the-second-world-war
Recycling for the war effort: www.keymilitary.com/article/waste-helped-win-war (by Austin J. Ruddy, 31 December 2020)
Pets: www.atlasobscura.com/articles/british-pet-massacre and www.iwm.org.uk/history/9-famous-animals-from-the-first-and-second-world-wars
Blackout accessories: www.butterflybalcony.com/2013/10/the-home-front-blackout-accessories.html

Other sources

Home Front Replica Pack (Memorabilia Pack Company, Edinburgh)
Women's War Replica Pack (Memorabilia Pack Company, Edinburgh)

Places to visit

Bletchley Park, Sherwood Drive, Bletchley, near Milton Keynes, Buckinghamshire, MK3 6EB
The Imperial War Museum, London, SE1 6HZ

Index

A Mile of Keys, Paddington, London 174

A Woman's Place – Now! leaflet 79

A.J. Waters Garage, Salisbury, Wiltshire 170

Admiralty, The 142

Air and sunshine 63

Air Ambulance Service (Flying Nightingales) 87

Air Raid Precaution Warden (ARP) 6, 70–73, 94, 168

Air raids 10, 13, 16, 44, 63, 70, 73, 122, 130, 139, 146, 150, 157–159

Air-raid shelters 13, 70, 73–76, 140, 159

Air Transport Auxiliary (ATA) 85–87, 171, 174

Allotments 10, 41–42, 71, 103

Aluminium 31, 141

Anderson shelter 71, 73, 134, 135, 159

Anti-Aircraft Command 79

Askey, Arthur, British comedian 92, 127

Auxiliary Territorial Service (ATS) 79–81, 153

Baby equipment and clothes 36, 68–69, 101, 106

Bacall, Lauren, film star 103

Ballroom dancing 120

Banns of Marriage 138

Battersea Dogs Home, London 163

Battle of Britain 10–11, 85, 143

Beech, Christine viii, 38

Bevin Boys 95–97

Bevin, Ernest, Minister of Labour 96

Bicks, Charity, GM 73

Biggin Hill Airfield, Kent 11

Blackout 4–6, 16, 64, 117, 129, 130, 145, 154–155, 163–165

Blackwell, Bette, Spitfire construction 170

Bletchley Park, Station X 8, 81, 92–93, 105, 147, 172

Blitz, The 2, 10, 14, 30, 42, 71, 73, 75, 124–125, 129, 130, 156, 159, 173

Board of Trade 106, 144

Bombs 6, 13, 33, 67, 72–74, 85, 120, 126, 159

Borough, Joan, Spitfire construction 172
Botting, Albert 'Lofty' viii 136–138
Botting, Joyce (née Thomas) viii, 115–116, 136–138
Bowen, Elizabeth, author 177
Boy Scouts 31, 60, 98, 142
Bread 23–24, 39–40, 44, 55, 149, 169, 176, 179
Breakfast cereal 169
British Army 25
British Broadcasting Corporation (BBC) 126, 128, 132, 173
British Overseas Airways Corporation (BOAC) 167
British Restaurants 55, 150
Brown, Jane, Heaton, Newcastle-upon-Tyne 170, 179–180
Buckingham Palace 40, 83, 141

Caged birds 159, 160, 163
Calais, France 172
Calories 36–37, 56
Canadian forces 172
Canning Town, London 174
Canteens 53–54, 76, 150–153
Cashman, Marion viii, 42, 111
Cats 4, 26, 158–161, 163, 178
Chatham Dockyard, Kent 29
Chattis Hill, secret Spitfire Factory, Wiltshire 171
Chickens 10, 41–45
Chislehurst Caves, Kent 76
Christmas, King's speech 131–133
Church 21, 131, 136, 138, 178
Churchill, Winston, Prime Minister 93, 103, 124, 161
Cinema 3, 47, 70, 79, 120, 122–125, 129
Civil Defence 94, 150
Civil Defence Leaflets (1939) 5–6
Civil Restaurants 54
Civilian Clothing Restriction Order (1942) 108
Clothes rationing 99, 108, 179
Coal 24, 32, 96, 178
Colossus computer 93
Community Kitchen 146
Connor, Kenneth, British actor 153
Conscription 77, 79, 94, 119
Cosmetics 36, 100, 113, 116
Cotton, Billy, band leader 126
County Herb Committees 60
Coupons and points 7, 30, 35, 38, 54, 57, 99–105, 108, 110, 111, 146, 170, 176, 179, 183
Coward, Noël, British film actor 122, 153
Crops 23, 41–42, 45
Crystal Palace FC 122

Dance halls 70, 120
David, Prince of Wales (King Edward VIII) 107, 131

D-Day landings, Normandy, France, June 1944 172
Denham, Lady, Director of Women's Land Army 104
Detling Airfield, Kent 84
Devon 25–26
Dickin Medal – animals' VC 159
Dietrich, Marlene, film star 103
Dig for Victory! 41, 177
Dior, Christian, fashion designer 181
Disney, Walt, US film animator 122
Dogs 4, 26, 158–162, 163, 164–165, 178
Doodlebug (German V1 flying bomb) 26
Double British Summer Time (DBST) 175
Dover, Kent 172
Driving Licence/Permit 7

East Anglia 90
East End (London) 28
Eggs, fresh, powdered/dried and shells 22, 36, 38, 41, 43, 45, 53, 57, 149, 169, 179
Electrical appliances 17
Elizabeth, the Queen 40, 83, 124
English Channel 172
English Football League 121
Enigma and Lorenzo code machines 93–94, 172–173
Entertainments National Service Association (ENSA) 126, 132, 153
Evening Despatch newspaper 143
Evening Standard newspaper 174
Exercise 163–164
Expeditionary Forces Institutes (EFI) 153

Factories and factory workers 3, 24, 31–32, 36, 42, 53, 65, 68, 74, 85, 90–92, 94, 99, 103, 116, 126, 142, 149, 154–155, 157, 170–171, 183
Farms and farm workers 10, 77, 88–90, 94, 103, 116, 120, 150
Fayre, Vivienne, ENSA casualty 153
Fields, Gracie, singer 92, 127, 153
Fire Brigade 77, 156
Fire-watching 71, 157
First Aid Nursing Yeomanry (FANY) 81
First World War (The Great War) 8, 17, 35, 41, 60, 69, 70, 81, 88, 126, 174
Fish, fishmonger, etc. 38, 57, 93, 154–155, 160, 177
Fleet Air Arm 83
Foden Motor Works band 132
Food Office 35–36, 47, 58
Forces Service (wireless station) 126

Formby, George, British film actor/comedian 122, 153
Fortnum & Mason, a London store 106
Fuel saving 24, 51, 54, 140, 144, 169

Gable, Clark, US film star 123
Gas mask 5, 8, 28, 53, 68–70, 74, 102, 105, 123, 140
George V 8, 131
George VI 8, 40, 67, 132–133, 156
Germany 25, 77, 128, 174
Gibson, Pamela, actress and Bletchley girl 125
Girl Guides 30, 60, 98, 110, 133, 142
GIs, Government Issue (American troops) 2–3, 16, 120, 151, 172
GIs' Instructions (handbook for US servicemen) 2–3, 31
Glasgow, Scotland 9
Glass 5, 21, 30, 131, 141, 145, 177
Glossop School Medical Officer/ sandwich 54
Good Housekeeping Magazine 24, 43, 107, 115
Good Night! Poster 74
Gorman, Linda (née Guess) 25–26
Government Bonds and National Savings Certificates 143
Government Code and Cypher School (GC & CS) 92
Gravesend, Kent 144
Greenwich Mean Time (GMT) 175
Guider magazine 133
Gurr, Frederick G., MBE, R & S Squad, London 156

Handley, Tommy, comedian 127
Harlequin sponge puddings manufacturer 168
Harrods, a London store 47, 131
Harthall, Harold, ARP Warden, Morden, Surrey 168
Hay box 51–53
Hepburn, Katharine, film star 103
His Majesty's Stationery Office (HMSO) 47, 62
Hitler 12, 14, 28, 64, 93, 128, 145, 148, 173
HMS *Chanticleer* 144
HMS *Whirlwind* 143
Holocaust, The 25
Home Companion magazine 20, 23, 65, 78, 145
Home Front 1, 79, 94, 113, 119, 123, 129, 150, 158, 186
Home Guard 42, 94, 155
Home Service (wireless station) 126
Horses, horse-power 10, 88, 133
Houses and housing 10, 17, 31–32
Housewife magazine (1940) 104

Housewife/wives 16, 20, 23–24, 47, 126, 149, 153, 177
How to be a Good Wife, school textbook (1954) 184
How to keep well in Wartime leaflet (1943) 61–62
Howard, Trevor, British film actor 122
Hudson, Valerie, showgirl 125
Hughes, Joan, ex-ATA pilot 174–175
Hyde Park, London 141
Hygiene 65

Idris soft drinks manufacturer 168
Illustrated magazine 159
Irish Sea 174
Isle of Wight 174

Jacquard, silk manufacturer 166
Jam and jam-making (jelly) 50, 58–61, 149, 179
Johns, Joan, laboratory tester at Spitfire factory 171
Johnson, Amy 87
Johnson, Celia, British film actress 122
Joyce, William, 'Lord Haw-Haw' 128

Keep Mum poster 146–147
Kent 25–26, 29, 42, 44, 76, 84, 138, 144, 172
Kindertransport 25

Labour Government 176, 179
Leeds, Yorkshire 29
Leigh, Vivien, British film actress 122–123
Lidell, Alvar, news reader 128
Limitation of Supply Order (1940) 36
Little, Mr., GM, Manchester 156–157
Liverpool 9, 29, 99
Livestock 30, 44
Local Defence Volunteers 26
London Underground (the Tube) 26, 29, 74–76
Lynn, Vera, singer 127, 153
Lyons Corner Houses 54

Magicians 172
Maidstone, Kent 25–26, 137
Make Do and Mend Campaign 111–112, 144, 163
Malnutrition 56
Mann, Richard, Walworth, East London 177–179
Marks & Spencer, High Street store 182
Mass Observation Survey 98–99
Meat 36, 38–39, 51, 57, 140, 141, 149, 177, 179
Merchant Navy 150–151
MI5, British Secret Service 172
Miles, Connie 11, 15, 28, 55, 81, 88, 130, 139, 148, 155, 160–161, 163, 170

Military Training Act (April 1939) 94
Milligan, Spike, British actor/comedian 153
Ministry of Agriculture 88
Ministry of Food 23, 35, 47, 51, 53, 58–59, 60,
Ministry of Fuel and Power 24
Ministry of Home Security leaflet 145
Ministry of Works 31–32
Money 8–9, 19–20, 25, 80, 105, 123, 130, 131, 139, 142–144, 146, 154–156
Morris Motor Manufacturing Company 119
Morrison shelter 74
Morrison, Herbert, Minister of Supply 141
Morton, Digby, fashion designer 151
Motor Driving Companies 81
Mrs Sew-and-Sew leaflets 144–145

National ARP Animal Committee (NARPAC) 158
National Anthem 13
National Health Service (NHS) (1947) 179
National Loaf (1941) 39–40
National Milk Scheme 36, 56
National Registration Identity Card (ID) 7, 35, 67–68, 70, 74, 105, 146
National Service (Armed Forces) Acts (1939, 1941) 77, 79, 94
National War Savings Committee 142
Navy, Army and Air Force Institutes (NAAFI) 151–153
Northfleet, Kent 44, 138
Norway 172
Nuffield, Lord 66, 119
Nuffield Trust 119
Nutrition & The War (1942) 37

Official Secrets Act 88, 93, 147, 171
Olivier, Laurence, British film actor 122
Operation Bodyguard 172
Operation Pied Piper 26

Paper 24, 93, 125, 128–129, 135, 140, 141
Pathe Newsreel 123
Patten, Marguerite 47, 50–51
Pearl Harbor, Hawaii 1
Pearson, Daphne, GM 84–85
Petrol (gas) 7, 121, 149, 154, 179
Petts Wood, Kent 29
Phoney War 26, 30

Pickles, Wilfred, 'northern' personality at the BBC 173–174
Picture Post magazine 168
Pigeons 173
Police 6, 77, 79, 97
Post Office or GPO 139, 155–156, 195
Post Office Savings Bank 143
Potato Pete 48
Potatoes 24, 42, 45, 47, 49, 79, 88, 134, 137, 149, 176
Prefabricated houses (Prefabs) 31–33
Publishing industry, London 129–130

Queue and queuing 3–4, 15, 35, 40–41, 146, 170

Radio Times magazine 126
Ration Book 7, 25, 35–36, 38, 53, 74, 105, 140, 146, 170
Rationing 6, 23, 34–37, 39–40, 50, 56, 58, 99, 108, 112, 121, 129–130, 134, 149, 154, 158, 160, 176, 179
Recipe: 'Fake' sausage rolls 134
Recipe: Bible cake 169
Recipe: Glossop health sandwich 55
Recipe: Lord Woolton's pie 49
Recipe: Mickey's dog biscuits 159
Recipe: Pilchard and cabbage spread 149
Recipe: Poor knight's fritters 149
Recipe: Rhubarb crumble 50
Recipe: Rosehip syrup 58
Recipe: Sadie's cheese omelette 53
Recipe: Toffee-coated nuts 134
Recycling 12, 31, 86, 111, 129, 140–141, 151, 160, 166, 174
Red Cross 125
Refuge Room 74
Registration Office 68
Reserved occupations 42, 77, 94
Rest Centres 139, 146, 150, 159
Robertson's marmalade manufacturer 168
Roosevelt, Eleanor, US First Lady 40
Rosehip syrup 58
Royal Air Force (RAF) 10–11, 84, 87, 106, 147
Royal Navy (RN) 12, 66, 109, 153, 163
Royal Society for the Prevention of Cruelty to
Animals (RSPCA) 160
Rubber 106, 108–109, 140–141
Russia 3, 90
Rutter, Stella, draughtswoman in Spitfire construction, High Post 171

Sailors' Mission, Swansea 132
Salvage crews 155

Salvation Army 54
Sanitary towels 65–66
School 25–26, 28–31, 47, 54–55, 57, 60, 79, 81, 92, 96, 102, 131, 142, 154–155, 163, 184–185
School of Army Experiments 79
Scotland 86, 94, 138, 172
Secret agents/spies 7, 68, 81, 88, 146–148, 172–173
Seelig, Manfred/Sherman, Martin 25
Selfridges, a London store 164–165
Sellers, Peter, British actor 153
Sheerness, Kent 174
Sheffield, Yorkshire 42, 54, 154
Shere, Surrey 11, 30, 55
Shops and shopping 7, 15–16, 25, 35, 37–38, 40–41, 65, 92, 98, 112, 124, 141–142, 146, 151, 154
Shoreditch, London 159
Signal and Transport Sections 83
Signal Office 83
Singer Sewing Machine Manual (1949) 183
Sleep 13, 63, 73, 83, 88
Smoking 63–64, 124
Soap 20–21, 23, 28, 36, 69, 116–117, 179
South Wales 29
Spam 39
Special Operations Executive (SOE) 81
Spitfires 10, 85–87, 143, 166, 170–171
St Leonard's Mothers Union, East Sussex 143
St Paul's Cathedral, London 10, 129
Starch 23
Stay-at-Home-Holiday Scheme 149–150
Steel and iron 73–74, 140–142, 174
Stepney, London 132
Sugar 1, 36, 50, 59, 134–135, 179
Suggested Menus for Holidays at Home leaflet 149
Sunlight Laundry, Salisbury, Wiltshire 170
Super Marine Spitfire factories, Southampton, Hampshire 170
Supply Pressed American Meat (Spam) 39
Swimming, dry 167
Sylvester, Victor, band leader 127

Tattoo beauty products 180–181
Tea 1, 21, 38, 73, 86, 88, 134, 140, 146, 148, 159, 179
Terry-Thomas, British actor 153
Thames Estuary 87, 174
The Bookseller magazine (1941) 129
The Daily Express newspaper 129

The Gardeners' Chronicle magazine (1939) 44
The Solent 174
The Times newspaper 129
Theatre 8, 87, 102, 119–121, 124–125, 127, 129, 172
Thomas, Amy viii, 25, 44, 138, 159
Topp, Gordon, telegram boy 171
Travel Permit 7

Uniforms 15, 80, 83, 86, 88, 92, 97–98, 102, 107, 110, 112, 121, 125, 132–133, 138–139, 151, 153–154, 166–167, 177, 181, 183, 190
US forces 172
US Lend-Lease Scheme 38, 176
US Marshall Aid Plan 179
Utility clothing/wear 108–111, 183
Utility Furniture Advisory Committee 33
Utility Furniture Catalogue (1943) 33

Vaccination 66
Vegetable Drugs Committee 60
Victory in Europe Day (VE day), May 1945 176
Victory over Japan Day (VJ day), August 1945 176
Vitamin Welfare Scheme 36, 56
Vogue fashion magazine 98, 103, 119

War Department, Washington DC 2
War Economy Standard Book Production (1942) 129
War Emergency – Information and Instructions leaflet (1939) 67–68, 70
Weather 4, 21–22, 71, 87–88, 100, 147, 178
Weekly Dispatch newspaper 28
Weekly ration
Weeks, Warship 142–144
Welfare Clinic 58
Welling, Kent 42
Wellworthies Spitfire Factory 171
Wessex Motor Works, Salisbury, Wiltshire 170
Wilkins-Ellis, Mary, ATA pilot 171
Wiltshire & Dorset Bus Co., Salisbury, Wiltshire 170
Windmill Theatre, London 125
Wireless/radio 3, 17, 47, 67, 83, 87, 92, 96, 119, 126–129, 131, 133, 140–141, 173–174
Women's Auxiliary Air Force (WAAF) 84
Women's Institute (WI) 60, 110, 145, 163

Women's Land Army, Land Girls 10, 79, 88–90, 104
Women's Royal Naval Service (Wrens) 81–84, 93, 167
Women's Timber Corps 90
Women's Voluntary Service (WVS) 29, 54, 102, 110, 142, 145, 150–151
Woolton, Lord (Minister of Food) 23, 47, 49–50, 56, 61, 161
Woolwich, the Arsenal 42

Yardley, cosmetics manufacturer 43, 113–134
Young Farmers Club 120